You Got This Girl

Overcoming Obstacles, Smashing Goals & Creating An Abundant Life

Cari Higham

You Got This Girl

Overcoming Obstacles, Smashing Goals & Creating An Abundant Life

Cari Higham
PO Box 454
Mayfield, Utah
84643

www.WhitandCariHigham.com

For speaking inquiries, permission requests, and bulk order purchase options, email whitney@whitandcarihigham.com.

ISBN: 9798546194536

Dedication

Whitney ~

For always believing in me, even when I don't believe in myself... For constantly pushing me to face my fears and go after my dreams... For supporting me and my crazy ideas, regardless of the outcome or income... For being my closest confidant, best friend and person I get to do life with.

Kaetz, Zandrix and Demzli ~

For being patient with mom during the times of chaos and unbalance... For loving me unconditionally... For giving me purpose, inspiration & joy.

Contents

Foreword

It is so perfect that Cari would write a book on a Mompreneur's Guide to Overcoming Obstacles, Smashing Goals and Creating an Abundant Life, because not only is she an expert at this subject but she did it!

You see, Cari created her own abundant life from below the ground up! (She will share all her secrets and goods in later pages.) I can't wait for you to hear all her crazy stories. LOL

Cari and I really got connected when she and her husband jumped into the world of network marketing, years ago.

She was eager to learn everything she needed to become a successful entrepreneur but as we all do, she ran into many roadblocks along the way.

AND this is where the REAL Cari was born!

She has always been an amazing person and an incredible mother, but she had more to give, more to create and more to do than I think she even knew at that time.

I have watched Cari's journey from the very beginning and it has been an absolute pleasure to work side by side with her all these years.

One thing about Cari is she's not afraid to challenge the norm. She is not afraid to ask the hard questions. Which has led her to come up with strategies and processes that are more effective and just WORK for entrepreneurs everywhere.

Especially busy ones that are not willing to sacrifice their family or relationships BUT still want and DESERVE it all!

Inside "You Got This Girl" you will get clear on how to pivot and get to YOUR success faster as an entrepreneur.

You will shed off the old you and the new you will come shining through by letting go of limiting beliefs.... towards time, money, mom guilt and comparitis.

Plus a few surprises that I will leave you to discover in the pages ahead on your own.

To sum it up, this book will completely change your life because you will never be the same once you meet Cari Higham.

Your life will be fuller and more complete.

She just does that to people.

Cari, I am so grateful our paths crossed and connected when they did. I absolutely treasure our friendship and our business adventures!

GIRL I am so DAMN proud of you! YOU my friend are a complete BADASS!

Brandy Shaver
Beach Boss Influencer

I met Cari and her husband, Whit at an online marketing event in May of 2018 where they were speakers and trained on stage. Purchasing a VIP upgrade for that event, I had the opportunity to network with them more intimately and got to know them better. We all totally hit it off and from there a friendship sparked.

One thing you'll learn about Cari is she's real, caring and personable.

Investing in my own mentorship and the same program she was in at the time, to level up my skill sets, I was able to spend more time with her and Whit, deepening our connection and friendship.

It wasn't long after I knew I needed to work with them because I wanted to build my business with my favorite people. Joining forces with our other business besties, we started our own company which we grew to multiple 7-figures in less than 18 months.

Not only has Cari been a huge help in guiding me as I've built a personal 6-figure business, but her expertise in limiting beliefs, evaluation and online marketing has also helped thousands of other entrepreneurs from around the globe create massive success.

This book is real, raw, bold and has no fluff. It's exactly what every Momprenuer needs to read if they want to rock their life and business.

Cari has mastered these skill sets that she has applied to her life and her business to create the ultimate life of abundance. She's invested in her own mentorship throughout her journey, becoming an expert, speaking on stage at Live events around the country, training 6-figure earners at private mastermind workshops, and has successfully built several 6 & 7-figure businesses.

What she spells out in You Got This Girl is what every entrepreneur will want to read so they can make those huge shifts needed to become successful in your life and business without having to sacrifice time with your family.

This book will definitely be a game changer for you especially if you have ever struggled with or currently struggle with building your business, raising your family, being a spouse, running the household,... all the things.

Cheers to your Success!!

Adrian Lindeen
Beach Boss Influencer

Have you ever had a crazy, big ass dream? The kind of dream you're almost afraid to share with people because they'll laugh at you, but you can't get it out of your mind?

Well I did... My professional career as a dentist was not fulfilling and so started my entrepreneurial journey back in 2015, full of drive and determination ...and then reality hit!

This wasn't as easy as I'd been told, far from it! And so those niggling doubts crept in and became louder and louder in my head until I began losing hope and my self belief hit rock bottom.

It wasn't long after that that I met Cari Higham and with her coaching and mentoring, I started to believe my dream wasn't as crazy as people were making it seem... She helped me see that it was possible and through that mentorship, she literally changed my life path!

With Cari's help, I went from ready to quit and give up on my dream, to building belief, overcoming the lack of confidence and building a business I love while making the money I always dreamt of making ... and on a path to making that crazy big ass dream a reality.

You Got This Girl will provide you with the tools necessary to make it happen for yourself as well... I firmly believe that every entrepreneur and aspiring entrepreneur out there needs to pick up a copy and read it several times to glean all the valuable diamonds of info that are in store for you.

Thank you Cari, from the bottom of my heart!

Fran Loubser
Beach Boss Influencer

I first met Cari at a network marketing conference in Las Vegas where she and her husband were speaking on stage.

I was truly impressed and touched by Cari's story. I could relate to every word she was saying... And the most important thing, she gave me hope and belief that I could also become successful in business and life while raising kids and having a full time job.

Cari has a unique ability to open your heart to possibilities, to get your mind focused on your goals despite the distractions and to give you the right tools and strategies to get noticed in the noisy social media world.

If you're a busy mom who is not yet ready to give up on her dreams, but is in need of real advice from someone who has walked in your shoes, then this is a must read! "You Got This Girl" is the breakthrough survival guide for aspiring mompreneurs...

Inside you'll dive deep into topics like mom guilt, work-life-balance, fear, dealing with haters, time management and so many other obstacles that tend to hold us back from accomplishing our dreams.

Plus, she shares her personal process and revolutionary "One-Hour-A-Day-System" to growing a thriving business that you will love, without sacrificing time and relationships with those that matter most to you.

The tools and processes you learn inside this book will change your life.

Kat Krasilnikoff
Beach Boss Influencer

Introduction

I don't consider myself anything or anyone special...

I wouldn't label myself as a "guru" or anything of that nature.

Yes, I've had a lot of success in a short period of time, but I come from humble beginnings...

And it definitely didn't happen overnight.

I'm a simple girl from a small town in Utah who dropped out of college at 19 to marry my best friend and love of my life...

And while I've NEVER regretted that decision, I have always had a dream of... More.

Maybe you can relate too...

A dream of more choices...

More time together...

More life experiences...

More impact.

Growing up I was a Jill of all trades and found myself hopping from job to job because I got bored... Or it didn't pay enough to keep me interested... Or I got sick and tired of being told what to do by my boss...

(I'm a little rebellious by nature and hate being bossed around.)

I worked in fast food, tried the receptionist and secretary thing twice, taught high school gym for a year, nannied, wrote articles for a newspaper, and went to beauty school and opened my own nail salon all before the age of 22...

And at the ripe age of 24 I had my first baby boy and still had no idea what I actually wanted to do with my life...

I only knew what I didn't want to do.

School wasn't an option... (I was an average student and we really couldn't afford it.)

And I wasn't confident enough in my talents to try my hand at an American Idol Audition or Hollywood movie casting! haha

So when my husband Whit was laid off from his career for the second time, and couldn't find a replacement anywhere because of advancing technology in his field... I knew that there had to be something better out there for us.

Because the Salon wasn't cutting it...

I had originally opened it with the hopes that I would have more control of my time and be present for my kids' as they grew up...

But what I actually found was that my salon ran me. If I didn't have a client sitting in the chair across from me, I wasn't making money.

The straw that finally broke the camel's back happened shortly after I went back to work after taking maternity leave when Kaetz, my oldest, was born. He was only a few months old and I had booked my calendar a little too full, not realizing I needed to plan more time in between appointments with a newborn.

I was behind schedule...

Towards the end of the day, Kaetz had lost it. He was hungry... He was tired... And when my last appointment of the day saw how frazzled I was trying to bounce Kaetz in his bouncer while filing her nails she said, "You better hurry and finish my nails so you can feed him."

Now, if that had happened today, I would have flipped this lady the bird and told her to find someone else to do her nails! LOL

But back then I was a people pleaser and much more soft spoken. I also couldn't afford to lose her as a client and my heart and soul was hurting. At that moment I realized having my own salon wasn't as glamorous as I thought it would be.

This led to an internal search and prayer for another job that would provide me with the lifestyle I craved...

One that allowed me the freedom to travel whenever we wanted, see my husband for more than an hour each night...

And the most important thing for me at the time, was to give me the ability to stay home with my children and be a loving and present mom in their lives as they grew up.

It was shortly after this that network marketing found me, and though it wasn't what I had in mind while praying for something different, it was the introduction I needed to personal growth and building something for myself that would create my own security in life.

But it didn't happen overnight. The struggle was very real in the beginning to find customers and build a team.

In fact, it took me 6 months to recruit my first person and my residual check sat around $80 after 2 years...

It wasn't until someone showed me how to attract and recruit people online that I finally started to get results...

Less than 10 months later, I was able to retire Whit out of his corporate job and I dove head first into the crazy, frustrating and beautiful world of digital entrepreneurship, where I discovered how to create the life I had always dreamed of living.

We'll dive deeper into that story a little later.

It's been 8 years since...

And I'm humbled to be sitting here writing this book... This love letter if you will... to you.

Over the years I've experienced heartache, grief, and have been so frustrated with my business at times I wanted to beat my head against the wall and call it quits...

Go find a 9-5...

And wallow in my own self pity because things weren't working the way I thought they should.

Yet, on the flip side...

Digital entrepreneurship has opened doors and brought me so much joy and happiness that I want to shout it out at the top of my lungs and have every mother that's sitting at home right now, surrounded by piles of bills and laundry hear my plea that there is a better way to live life.

My greatest hope with this book... is that you take something from it that will keep you fighting the good fight.

To make you a more resilient entrepreneur...

To help you begin to believe in yourself...

To share some concepts and processes with you that have been the key to me building multiple 6 & 7-figure businesses online over the last few years.

To prepare you for the inevitable changes that come with entrepreneurship, allowing you to be more flexible and adaptable.

(As my good friend Ross Gellhar from Friends would say... PIVOT! LOL)

And to give you the space you need to feel deep down in your soul that God, the Universe, whatever you want to call it, wants YOU to be successful.

That you finish this book ready to attack your goals and manifest your biggest dreams into existence...

And then take intentional action to make it happen.

Because you and me... We're both a different breed of human.

We want more.

We crave more.

And we think a lot differently than most people.

And one of my favorite things about entrepreneurship is that it doesn't discriminate.

Regardless of where you come from... Regardless of age, gender, race... And regardless of who you were in your past, you CAN be successful and accomplish the dreams and big ass goals you've set for yourself.

My question to you is, how quickly do you want to get there and accomplish your dreams? Or are you happy to remain stuck and complacent in spinning your wheels?

Because I've made so many mistakes... Mistakes that could have been easily avoided had I been equipped with the right tools and processes ahead of time. And these mistakes ended up costing me precious time, money and energy.

I want to help you fast track your success to help you avoid making these same mistakes... And see you rise to the top and create your own freedom in your life.

And by the time you finish "You Got This Girl", you'll have the tools, concepts & processes in your back pocket that will keep you in the game longer, help you pivot when needed, and get you to YOUR success faster than you can imagine.

All while being there for the people that matter to you most.

Welcome to my world. You're in for a ride!

Chapter 1: Being Successful Is A Choice

You get what you choose.

It's always fascinating to me that 2 people, with the same level of education, influence or skill sets can start a program or a journey at the exact same time...

Have all the same resources available to them...

And one person will succeed while the other quits or never seems to get any traction.

What causes this?

Why do some people thrive while others fail?

In March 2016 I found a mentor and I invested in myself for the very first time. I knew I needed to up my skill sets and learn a new strategy to grow my business using Social Media.

The cost of the program was $3,000 for 12 months.

I had to use that year's tax return to invest in the program, because at the time, we were broke and usually, we would use our tax return to live on.

That money went toward things like buying groceries, paying off bills, etc. So it was a big deal for us to use our return on something different.

We had been living with our parents for almost 2 years at that point and it was one of those times in our life when we were as low as we could get.

Whit was bringing home about $1650 a month after taxes and our baby boy Zandrix was still in diapers. I was trying to get our business off the ground with no luck. Bringing in a whopping $80 a month was all I had to show for my hard work and the adversary was working on me hardcore to give up on my business and just go get a job.

But I knew this program was the answer to me finding success. I could feel it in my gut. So with tears streaming down my cheeks, hands shaking and voice quivering... Because I knew I was taking a huge gamble on myself in doing this... I read off our credit card number and paid the $3,000 to get started.

Later that day we had to make a run to the grocery store and when we got there we decided to divide and conquer...

Whit took 1 boy to go grab diapers and I went to grab a few grocery essentials we were out of with the other boy.

Now, before I go further... You need to understand how I would shop at the time.

There had been 2 shopping trips prior to this one where I had made it to the cash register and didn't have enough money to pay for the groceries I had in my cart... Resulting in me having to take certain items back to the shelf and asking the cashier to take items off the belt because I couldn't pay for them.

It was embarrassing... So to save myself the humiliation of it happening again, I started rounding groceries up to the nearest dollar.

So if a can of soup cost 76 cents... I would round up to $1... If a gallon of milk was $2.38, I would round up to $3. This way I always knew I had enough money to pay for everything in my cart when I went to checkout.

The day I paid the $3,000, Whit met me in the bread aisle with 2 boxes of diapers... And as he sat them in the cart he said, "They've gone up 5 dollars a box."

My heart sank as I looked over all the items in my cart... Evaluating how much everything was going to cost us... And slowly, I turned and put the 2 loaves of bread I had in my hands back on the shelf, because I knew we weren't going to be able to pay for them.

That's how I started that $3,000 program... At that moment, I made the choice that I was going to change our situation.

No matter how hard it got... No matter how much I wanted to quit... I was going to be successful and retire Whit out of his job. A job that he hated, and the day would come that I would walk into Walmart or Costco and not look at a single price tag because I wouldn't care about cost.

There were several other aspiring entrepreneurs that started this $3,000 program the same time I did.

Once a week we'd hop on Zoom calls with our mentors to see what was working for each other, to get feedback and to hold each other accountable until the next week.

I noticed that as the weeks progressed, certain people would hop on these calls in a different headspace than me... They'd whine about things not working...

They'd complain about things they thought were holding them back... Or the things they thought they still needed to have in order to be successful.

And one by one they'd stop showing up for the accountability Zooms and would quit.

A lot of these people were better off than me starting out too... They definitely weren't having to put their bread back on the shelf at the grocery store. A few of them even had prior success and plenty of influence getting started...

So why did the majority of them fail & quit while I went on to break through my first $10,000 month 7 months into the program?

The answer is simple. I *CHOSE* to be successful.

I made that choice by showing up everyday and taking action.

I chose to focus on the good things that were happening while going through the program. If something was unclear or not available or not easy to find while going through videos and trainings, I chose to get resourceful and figure out a way to make things work...

While others chose to blame, complain and stay stuck.

Now don't get me wrong... I care a lot about those people I went through the program with... Some of them are still dear friends to this day.

But if there's anything I've learned over the years, it's that you get what you focus on... Literally. LITERALLY!

And you get what you choose to see.

If you try to find the bad in anything you're doing... Starting a new program... Building your business... Your relationships... Anything in your life... You will find it.

And as you search for the things that aren't working or things you're lacking, more and more of those things will manifest themselves to you until you feed yourself full of lies, excuses and plain ol' dirt that will cloud your mind and deceive your judgment.

You'll start to feed your limiting beliefs even more with phrases like, "See, I knew this wouldn't work. I knew I wouldn't be successful. This is a scam. I'm not good at this. I'm not good at that. Maybe I'm not cut out for this thing."

On the flip side...

If you choose to focus on the positive. If you choose to focus on and find the good in what you're doing, you'll find it.

And as you search for things that ARE working in a program... Your business... Your relationships... Your life... More and more positive things, good, and wins will manifest themselves to you.

Keeping that open mind space will kick in the resourceful side of your brain which will allow solutions to flow freely to you... And that's when the results start to happen.

It all comes down to a choice.

Going back to that $3,000 program... When I look back at what resources I had available to me at the time, the program was newer. Only ONE email was sent to me to get me started. I didn't have a step-by-step roadmap to follow to help me get results. I had to figure a lot of stuff out on my own. (I'm grateful for that because it forced me to be resourceful... A skill set I lacked before this experience.)

But because I chose to find the good in it... Because I chose to dig in and get to work... Because I chose to advocate for my business and reach out to my mentors... Because I chose to make that program work for me... And because I chose to be resourceful and find answers to things in other places when needed... I rose to the top.

I changed our circumstances... I got us out of the basement... I retired my husband from his job in less than a year...

And you can do it too...

But you have to *choose* to make it happen... And you have to continue to choose to make it happen in your actions every day.

It's in my nature to mentor and lead with care and concern... When working with my students, teammates and clients I always speak from my heart in hopes to build you up, inspire you and equip you with the tools you need to be successful.

But the second you start whining, complaining or blaming other people, situations or circumstances for you not getting results, I have no sympathy and will turn it around right back to you.

As hard as it is to hear... Your lack of results or not being where you want to be right now is on you. No one else is to blame.

There are people out there who have had it bad... Worse than me... Worse than you... And they've worked through that baggage to rise to the top.

You didn't have a good childhood? You were beaten? You were raped? You've experienced loss? You've seen and experienced horrible things?

I feel for you... My heart goes out to you... Don't think for one second I don't care... But make the choice right now to move past it. Whether you believe it or not YOU ARE WORTH IT!

Ask yourself, "What might I do to heal from this, to let it go, and to move forward?" Then go out and DO IT!

You've always had the choice to be successful... And you always will. Never allow anything to define your worth or allow anything to hold you back from your dream.

*****

So how do you stay in a positive headspace and continue to take action when you feel like you've exhausted resources? When you feel like nothing is working? When you're having a bad day?

One thing you need to understand is you are a human being with emotions... Complicated, beautiful, intense emotions that play a huge role in your thoughts, actions and habits.

If you try to grow a business solely focused on how you "feel", you can quickly and easily get stuck, make poor choices and not get anywhere or gain traction.

For the past few years I've helped facilitate Social Media workshops for digital entrepreneurs, helping them grow & scale their businesses to the 6 & 7-figure mark.

With the help of my business partners, we end each day of these workshops with an evaluation process asking 3 specific questions that effectively help us make decisions.

What worked?

What didn't work?

What might I do differently?

Through this process, we've continued to refine the workshops and make them more effective for our students...

These questions rely on externally verifiable data (things we can see with our own eyes & prove happened) to determine whether something is working or not working with the workshops...

Whit & I have also taken this evaluation process and have used it at the end of each day in our own business.

We specifically break it down to 3-2-1...

What are 3 things that worked today?

What are 2 things that didn't work?

And out of the 2 things that didn't work, what is 1 thing we might do differently tomorrow to get closer to the desired result we want?

Now, I didn't invent this process of evaluation... I learned it from my own mentors Blair and Melissa Dunkley several years ago...

But this evaluation process has made taking action in our business much more effective because we don't rely on feelings or emotions to make decisions. We use the externally verifiable data to determine what changes need to happen to get closer to the results we want.

And when we do make a change, we use the data to see if it worked or not.

It all comes down to testing and keeping our emotions at bay while we make decisions.

Now, how might you apply this process to your own business?

An example might be after meeting with a prospective customer, teammate or client, you'll ask yourself the 3-2-1...

What are 3 things that worked about that meeting? What are 2 things that didn't work? What is 1 thing I might change when meeting with my next prospect that will help the meeting run smoother or end in the desired result I want?

You might be tempted to fall back on "feelings" when going through the process...

When asking what worked you might be tempted to say "Nothing worked. I didn't get the sale. They didn't join my team. They don't want my services. Nothing is working."

In order for something to not work, you would have had to do nothing to begin with. Having the meeting in itself is something that worked. So push yourself to find 3 things that worked with that meeting.

You might also find that when you ask what didn't work, you want to throw out a list of things that went wrong, which can easily spiral into more negative feelings that keep you closed off to the possibility of change or growth.

To keep this from happening, I like to ask What are the 2 MAJOR things that didn't work about the meeting?

This will keep you focused on only 2 things, which means you can look at your meeting in a more positive mind space.

And, only focusing on 2 things also makes it easier to choose the 1 thing you'll do differently or change for the next meeting.

After you do your next meeting, you'll run through the 3-2-1 again and see if the change you made moved you closer to your desired result.

This evaluation process is the fastest and most effective way I've personally found to get results and develop the skill sets you need for success in your particular niche.

The faster you can apply this process and take action after each evaluation, the quicker your business will grow.

So I challenge you to use it after every action you take in your business from here on out.

Do a Live Video?

Ask the 3 questions.

Make a tweak to an ad?

Ask the 3 questions.

Have a conversation with a prospect about your business?

Ask the 3 questions.

Action without evaluation will keep you stuck and frustrated.

The most amazing part is that this process can work in every area of your life... Not just your business.

In your marriage, your relationship with your kids, learning a new skill, how you communicate with others, etc.

What are 3 things that are working?

What are 2 major things that are not working?

What is 1 thing I might do differently or change?

So remember you have a choice to make things work. You have a choice to rise to the top in your business. You have a choice to overcome obstacles and let go of the baggage that might be wearing you down or holding you back. You have a choice to change your circumstances and make life better for yourself.

Because one thing is for sure... You won't be handed your dream on a silver platter. You cannot find a happy life. It is not something you can trip and fall into. You have to create it for yourself!

Now you have a process to help you do that.

Yes, sometimes crap happens and life will never go as planned...

The difference between happy and successful people... And people that are unhappy and wallowing in self-pity, is how you CHOOSE to handle the crap when it's thrown at ya.

Sometimes systems glitch... Sometimes people are mean... Sometimes business deals fall through... Sometimes relationships end... Sometimes tragic moments change the trajectory of our lives forever...

But if you CHOOSE to play the victim... Because it is a choice.... If you CHOOSE to allow circumstances to define who you are and what you deserve...

Then you'll ALWAYS BE STUCK in a never-ending loop of blaming and shaming other people and things you can't control for things you have a CHOICE to move past and overcome.

Choose to take responsibility for yourself, your actions and your behavior. When you take responsibility, you're in control... And that's a pretty cool thing...

Because that's when you have the POWER to decide how your life plays out and you have the POWER to change your situation and circumstances.

It really comes down to you making a choice.

So don't allow crappy situations and circumstances to determine whether or not you get the results you want in your business and out of this life.

Because those situations and the choices other people make will never have control over you... Unless you allow them to.

So get out there, take action, evaluate, and choose to look for the good in all you see, hear and do and success will follow.

Chapter 2: Being Successful Isn't A Sin

I got my entrepreneurial spirit from my dad...

You see, he was an insurance salesman most of my life... And he was a damn good one at that.

He was an independent contractor and made his own rules. He called the shots and determined when and where he was going to work and that meant he had a lot of flexibility with his time.

Looking back, I'm proud of him. He provided a good life for his family and watching him, I saw a tenacious work ethic in action.

I'm blessed to have had his example to look up to in my own entrepreneurial journey.

However, the thought of being an entrepreneur and working for myself was tainted a little when I was younger because of a few things that happened in my childhood...

So I never really thought entrepreneurship was the direction I wanted to go.

Growing up, we definitely never went without... But we lived a very modest lifestyle.

We had a nice home, but it wasn't a mansion by any means...

We had a camper, but no boat or 4-wheelers or other toys that a lot of my friends' parents had...

My mom always shopped clearance sales and having 5 kids, there were more than enough hand me downs to keep us clothed, so I never really had the new flashy outfits like my friends.

I remember going to a family dinner at my dad's twin sister's house when I was around the age of 7. All 6 of my dad's brothers and sisters were there with their families.

As I sat in the garage, listening to my dad and his siblings crack jokes and talk about life, my Uncle Doug, who was my dad's business partner at the time, turned to me and asked, "Do you think you'll work in sales when you grow up?"

To which I replied, "No, I don't want to be poor."

Everyone laughed... But shortly after, my dad pulled me outside and we had a heart-to-heart that I remember vividly to this day.

He said, "Cari, you hurt me with your comment about working in sales. What makes you think we're poor?"

I told him about our modest lifestyle... How I always had hand me downs while my friends had new... How they had video games, 4-wheelers, and other "material things" that I thought meant their parents were rich and somehow better off than us.

He patiently listened to me express my frustration of feeling "less than" my friends...

I even remember getting a little emotional because I felt unworthy as I listed the things they had and I didn't...

Then he said, "I see where you're coming from. It can be hard feeling like you don't have everything you want... But you're forgetting a few things... How many vacations have we been on that you can remember?"

I thought for a minute and started listing them...

Disneyland several times and Sea World several times, camping, Moab, week long road trips to more places than I could count...

Weekend getaways as a family to swim, hike or see some type of historical site...

The zoo, Lagoon, St. George...

I immediately felt happiness as we talked about all the fun we'd had as a family in my short lifetime.

He then said, "Cari, your mom and I don't measure wealth by the amount of 'things' we have. We would much rather spend our money on memories and experiences with you kids. Because we love each of you so much and at the end of the day, things wear out or break... But the memories we make with each other will be there with you the rest of your life."

At that moment, I thought differently about what "creating wealth" meant... And I never again judged how much money someone made or how successful they were by the size of their house or the type of car they drove.

And my longing for materialistic things was replaced with a love of travel, adventure and creating experiences with those I love.

Today, Whit and I too live a pretty modest lifestyle. Our home isn't anything grand and from the outside, many wouldn't think we are as well off as we are from our lack of "things"...

But I personally know 6 & 7-figure earners that live paycheck to paycheck because they have more "things" than they can afford.

If you find yourself looking at other people's lives and longing to have the things that they have... Remember that at the end of the day, things are just things...

Never judge how much someone makes by the car they drive or the house they live in...

Because it's much more important to be smart when creating your wealth.

Live beneath your means and put your money to work for you, so that more wealth can be created.

Now, don't think for one second I'm telling you getting a new car, or wanting the toys and a big house is bad. There's nothing wrong with wanting materialistic things!

If something materialistic will give you the motivation to get off your butt and work your business to be able to afford it then, girl, go for it! I myself drive a Red Lincoln Navigator... It was the car I had on my vision board when I first started my business and it was part of the motivation I needed to get to work.

But remember, at the end of the day, things can wear out or break...

But how you treat people, memories and life experiences you create are far more valuable and will last a lifetime and beyond.

And your "worthiness" is NOT tied to the amount of money you make or the things you have.

******

It wasn't long after this family dinner with my dad's family that my dad started a new venture...

He started working with a man to build a new Life Insurance Agency in the State of Utah.

The deal was, if my dad helped him build this agency into a multi-million dollar company... If he and my dad's brother Doug met certain goals over the next 5 years, then this man... We'll call him Sam... Would make my dad and Doug partners and they would own and run the company together.

With this deal and goal in mind, my dad got to work building... He knew this would mean financial security and wealth for our family.

He had clients all over Utah and that meant long days away from our family.

This time in my life was hard... I was used to having my dad around... And we were going weeks at a time not seeing him. He would be up and out of the house before we were awake... And he would get home late at night when we were asleep.

I remember my mom comforting my little sister one night as she cried herself to sleep because of how much she missed him.

It was hard on us all...

But, after what seemed like forever, my dad finally did it.

He built the company from the ground up, qualified for President of the President's Club as a top producer of the nationwide company that he represented, and was excited to finally be named partner of the agency.

Finally, the day arrived that my dad had been working so hard toward for 5 years...

I was 11 at the time... And one morning, Doug knocked on my dad's office door and asked my dad if he could speak to him. My dad invited him in and as he sat down, Doug told my dad that the partnership they'd been hustling to earn... After surpassing every goal and expectation in the last 5 years to make them a partner... Was over.

Sam had decided to make his son a partner, instead of my dad and Doug.

Sam had gone back on his word... He went back on his deal.

All my dad's hard work... All the miles and hours in the car... All the time he'd given up with his kids over the last 5 years... For nothing.

After Doug left my dad's office my dad sat looking out his window feeling defeated.

With anger, frustration and sadness, he said 10 words, "Heavenly Father, is there anything more to life than this?"

Now you need to remember my dad was the top producer... Nothing happened in the agency without my dad being behind it. He recruited and trained and met with everybody's clients in training. Every associate wanted my dad to work with them.

Within a week of Doug entering my dad's office and my dad saying those 10 words, everything that he was working on began to come apart and crumble to the ground.

He sat in his office wondering what was happening and why everything he had worked so hard for, the past 5 years to build, was coming apart at the seams. He became so discouraged from everything coming apart and no longer being able to trust Sam, that both my dad and Doug decided to leave the firm.

He packed our family up, moved us 200 miles south to the center of the state and we started over.

The next few years were a challenge for our family as finances were extremely tight...

However, my dad was resilient and tenacious... And because he worked from home, I was able to watch as he got things off the ground and slowly, but surely, he and my mom rebuilt their life from the ground up.

Through years of focusing on personal growth and growing my own mindset, I discovered something about myself...

Because of watching my dad go through this experience, I developed a belief that being an entrepreneur meant life was going to be feast or famine for my own family if I chose to follow in my dad's footsteps...

I remember being upset and questioning God myself... "Maybe God really didn't want people to be wealthy," I thought...

"What was the point of working hard and building something if he was just going to take it away? Maybe money really does bring out the bad in people."

Do you find yourself asking these same questions? Do you find yourself with the same beliefs?

"Maybe God doesn't want me to be successful."

"I haven't done anything to be worthy of creating wealth."

"I can't build something myself, because it could easily fall apart... And then what?"

"God doesn't want me to be wealthy."

"Money is bad."

"Wanting to build wealth is bad."

"Trying to build wealth takes my focus off of God."

Girl, I could go on forever...

Over the past few years coaching entrepreneurs, I've found that there is something frequently taught in many religions that keeps a lot of people stuck.

They teach that you should "Be Happy With Where You're At." I get what they're trying to accomplish by saying this...

Happiness is a choice and you can choose to be happy now, regardless of finances or circumstance. I get that and it's absolutely true.

But, many people hear this and take it to mean that God doesn't want them to strive for more.

That they need to accept where they're at and not push to become better.

And in many instances, being a wife and mom means you're supposed to sit at home and clean and take care of kids and put your own goals, dreams and desires on the back burner.

I'm here to tell you this is NOT what it means.

Absolutely, be happy and find joy in your journey, but do not for one second think it means that you have to be content with where you're at... Especially if you aren't happy because of your circumstances.

There is nothing wrong with wanting more... There is nothing wrong with wanting to create a life for your family that includes materialistic things, more vacations, more activities, more time and more experiences.

There is nothing wrong with wanting to create wealth.

In fact, the Lord WANTS you to be successful. He wants to bless you with all you desire.

I remember in December 2015, Whit met with our Bishop for tithing settlement. This is a meeting that happens at the end of each year with your ward Bishop to go over how much money you donated that year and declare whether it was a full tithe of 10%, a partial tithe, or lower.

I stayed home with our boys since our baby Zandrix wasn't feeling well.

We were living in Whit's mom's basement at the time, trying to get our business off the ground...

In fact, we had been trying to grow our team for 2 years with no success and my prayer every day was that things would finally take off... Finances would get better... I'd be able to retire Whit... And we'd get out of the basement and be able to finally get a house of our own.

Whit walked in after meeting with our Bishop and called me downstairs... He showed me how much we had paid that year in tithing and my jaw hit the floor.

Even though we didn't have much to give to begin with, the amount written on that piece of paper was nowhere near what it should have been. I wouldn't even call it a partial tithe.

In that moment, I felt we had robbed the Lord and the guilt I felt from all the prayers I'd said asking for the Lord to take care of us when we weren't even willing to take care of others was a punch in the gut.

We made a promise that day that we would never fall short again... Whether we felt we had the means or not we would always donate 10% of everything we made to the poor and needy.

And since that day, tithing has been the first thing we pay with each check that comes into our account.

Call it coincidence, call it divine power, call it opening our minds to abundance, whatever you want...

The second we started trusting the Lord and donating 10% of everything we made to build up the kingdom and help those in need... Our income started to grow.

In fact, it was 11 months later we had our first $10,000 month.

Now I want you to think for a minute about how much money 10% is off a 6 or 7-figure income.

That's quite a chunk of change we've donated over the past few years...

How many lives have been blessed because of that donation?

I don't share this to boast or brag... but for you to see what a blessing money is to others.

Without money, you're really only able to bless the lives of and help those you come into direct contact with...

And while I hope you do this anyway, the ripple effect can take time to bless hundreds or thousands of people when you can only help with your own 2 hands.

When you have money, you're able to bless the masses quickly.

When there's natural disasters, it takes money to send in supplies and relief to those that are suffering.

It takes money to run non-profits and other charities.

It takes money to save women and children from sex trafficking around the world.

It takes money to build water wells for villages in Africa.

It takes money to be able to feed starving children in 3rd world countries...

I hope you get the idea by now.

Don't you think the Lord wants to bless you so that you can bless others? Of course he does!

Money is NOT evil...

And even the Love of Money is not evil.

The Lord uses regular people like you and me to run his errands and to build his kingdom every single day.

You're an instrument in his hands. And when you think abundantly and use money to bless others, he rewards you with more than you can imagine.

Now you might be wondering whatever happened to Sam... The guy that backstabbed my dad...

Well, fast forward about 15 years from when my dad left the agency...

My dad got a letter in the mail from an attorney stating that Sam was in big trouble...

Turns out, not long after my dad left the firm, Sam started doing things with his client's money that the IRS considers "illegal"... And over the next several years embezzled millions of dollars of his clients' money and it had finally caught up with him.

On record as one of the biggest ponzi schemes to ever go down in the State of Utah, Sam was sentenced to live the rest of his life in prison.

Obviously, my dad was innocent and would have never taken part in anything like this, but I want you to consider and think about the timing of it all...

What are the chances my dad would be forced to leave the agency and make a change just before all the illegal actions of his partners would start taking place?

Think about my dad staring out the window asking the Lord, "Is there anything more to life than this?" The pain he felt... The emotions flowing through him to see everything he had worked so hard and sacrificed so much to build, slipped through his fingers.

I like to think that in that moment, when my dad was staring out the window, broken, God was whispering back, "Yes there is... And because I love you, I'm forcing you to pivot."

When big illegal things like this go down, whether you did it or not, you can be guilty by association.

My dad was forced to pivot and change direction at a time that he couldn't possibly be blamed or found guilty in any of the illegal and wrong doings of Sam and his son.

God's timing is always perfect.

My dad looks back and the blessings that came from Sam going back on his word are too many to count... A few including:

Being able to be home and present with his family again...

Knowing he had the skill sets, resources and connections to be able to pivot and make the change he did for his family...

Not going to prison... He's so grateful he didn't go to prison! LOL

If you find yourself in a position where you're frustrated, sad or even angry at God asking "Why Me?"

Remember Sam...

God loves you... He wants you to be successful... And you might not know why you're going through what you're going through right now...

But God's timing is perfect. And just like a diamond is formed under extreme heat and pressure... So are you.

One day your story will all make sense... And you'll be stronger, in a better place, and surrounded by more blessings than you can imagine because of it... And God will be there whispering, "Because, I love you."

"No one can be you, better than you."

-Cari Higham

Chapter 3: The Poison That Will Kill Your Business

Whit invited me to start going to the gym with him in the fall of 2018...

Our 2nd boy Zandrix was 3 years old at the time and I was looking to strengthen and tone a few areas of my body...

Really, I'd been whining and complaining about the "fluffiness" I'd put on since having both boys, the "mom pooch" was in full effect, and I was the heaviest I'd ever been.

Now I've always lived a fairly healthy lifestyle...

I eat okay and being a runner most of my life, I can easily run circles around most people, but running a mile 4-5 days a week wasn't cutting it anymore.

Walking into the gym I felt right at home looking at the elliptical and treadmill and I was pushed way out of my comfort zone picking up that pair of dumbbells for the first time.

Since I had never lifted weights a day in my life, I knew there was going to be a learning curve.

However, Whit was a great teacher and I was feeling the burn and ache in my muscles right away.

Excited about the end result I was after, I was committed and believed that with the right routine and diet I'd be back to my pre-baby self in no time.

Several weeks went by and I was slowly adding more weight to my workout...

I'd gone from a 5 pound bicep curl to a 10 pound...

From barely being able to lift the bar on the bench press to adding an additional 10 pounds...

And I was able to do more than 5 reps on each step of my routine each day.

I was making progress and getting closer and closer to my desired weight and waist size each day and I was excited about that progress.

One specific morning I got to the gym early, had been at it for a few minutes and was feeling pretty good...

I could feel the swelling in my arms and pretty much felt like those pictures you see of Arnold Schwartzenegger from back in the day when he was in his body building prime.

I was dripping in sweat and I could see my veins pulse as I ripped through my bicep curls.

I was on top of the world and felt like I could fight anyone that walked through the doors at that moment...

(Totally kidding. I'm not a violent person and have never fought anyone a day in my life! haha)

But just as I was on a major adrenaline high from my workout and was feeling great, a gal I know that had been going to the gym for years walked in...

We'll call her Ash.

Ash walked over to my area, smiled at me as she picked up the 25 pound dumbbells and started warming up into her own bicep curls.

After a few pumps she set down the 25's and picked up the 30 pound dumbbells...

Again, she breezed through her curls like they were nothing before setting them down to pick up the 35 pounders.

I looked down at my own 10 pound dumbbells in my hands and I suddenly felt silly.

Do you remember the episode of Spongebob Squarepants when Sandy Squirrel enters Spongebob into an anchor throwing competition?

At one point in that episode, Spongebob flexes his biceps only for them to droop into a letter U...

Signifying that he's a wimp and there was obviously no way he could win the competition against all the big fish and sharks he was competing against.

That's how I felt.

I was Spongebob.

I felt defeated... And was embarrassed to be in her presence.

How could I seriously become as good as Ash?

Her arms were chiseled.

She had the body I dreamed of having.

Looking at myself in the mirror I forgot about all the progress I had made in those few weeks and began questioning if lifting weights was for me.

I can hear your thoughts right now...

"Girl, what are you thinking? You can't compare yourself to her! She'd been going to the gym for years! Look at all the progress you'd made... You can't give up! Believe in yourself!"

It's funny how our brains will try to talk us out of things when we're uncomfortable... Our brains crave comfort and want to keep us safe at all times...

But Brian Tracy once said, "Move out of your comfort zone. You can only grow if you are willing to feel awkward and uncomfortable when you try something new."

I'm curious, how often have you done this to yourself?

Especially in your business?

You get going... Developing your skill sets... Taking action to get a desired result...

And then someone comes up to the side of you and starts doing what you're doing faster... Better...

They have the business you dream of. Or they're just getting started and overnight they're a success...

While you're in the trenches, hitting what seems like every obstacle imaginable...

You start asking yourself, "What the heck is wrong with me? Why is it easy for them and I'm struggling? How can I compete with them? They've been doing this forever. They're so good at everything they do. I can't compete. Maybe entrepreneurship isn't for me."

It's my turn to give you the pep talk...

"Girl, what are you thinking?! Knock that shit off... You can't compare yourself to her! She's been in business way longer than you have. She's been developing her skill sets for years... Look at all the progress YOU'VE made! There's no such thing as an overnight success! Don't give up on yourself! You Got This!"

Anytime you start something new, you'll be the new kid on the block... And entrepreneurship is not exempt from that.

And even those people that have immediate success when they first start as an entrepreneur didn't just "get lucky."

I remember when we first took our business online, I'd look at some of the industry leaders' pages I was following and was envious of the thousands upon thousands of followers they had...

Meanwhile, I had less than 100...

I felt a lot like Spongebob Squarepants back then...

Tiny...

Small...

A nobody in my industry yet...

But I got to work and stayed persistent...

And consistent...

And before I knew it, I had 1,000 followers...

And then 5,000...

And then 10,000...

Our business was growing faster and faster the more consistent and persistent I was...

And now, we have a following that beats some of the "gurus" I envied for so long.

So how do you stay in your lane and continue taking action, while keeping the comparitis at bay so it doesn't take over? Because comparitis is a poison that will keep you stuck in your business and in life.

The best advice I ever got was from a mentor and now dear friend of mine in 2017, right before my business really took off.

She said, "The only person you're allowed to compare yourself to is the person you were yesterday... And if you are going to compare yourself to someone else - because it's human nature and even the best find it hard to avoid - make sure you're comparing your behaviors with their behaviors... And not their results with your results."

Friend, everyone is on a different journey in both entrepreneurship and life...

It's not fair for you to compare your results with anyone because you don't know what God-given talents they had starting out... Or what their back story was before jumping into entrepreneurship.

So if someone is getting the results you want, then take a look at what they're DOING every day to get those results.

If you focus on being intentional about your own behaviors, and work to develop your skill sets to execute those behaviors effectively, you'll naturally get the same results that person is getting over time.

And one thing is true...

You yourself have God-Given Gifts that the world needs you to share. And no one can be you, better than you.

So stay in your lane... Strive to do and be a little better each day... Focus on developing your skill sets and be consistent and persistent.

The results will follow.

Now you might be wondering how my gym journey turned out.

Well, after I was done with that workout I went home and Whit gave me the same pep talk I just gave you. He breathed life back into me... So I decided to keep at it.

He's customized my workouts and meal plans to my body type and the results I was looking to get over the past 3 years...

I started comparing how I was lifting my weights to how Ash lifted hers... How often she went to the gym... And how long her workouts were compared to my own...

Her warm up and cool downs to my own warm up and cool downs...

Basically, her behaviors to my own behaviors.

And over time, with consistency and intentional action, I started to achieve milestones and the results I wanted when I first started out.

Even after having my 3rd baby, during the pandemic when our gym was closed, not being able to go lift for months at a time...

I just hit a huge goal for myself and am back down to the size I was before Whit and I got married.

But more important than the weight, I've learned to judge my own progress by how I feel, how I look in the mirror, and by how my clothes fit.

When you have a plan for success and combine it with consistency and persistence, magic happens...

Businesses grow, relationships build, and you get "ripped" at the gym...

Don't compare your results to someone else's...

Instead, compare yourself to the person you were yesterday and try to do and be a little better.

Embrace the amazing person and gifts you have and remember...

You Got This Girl.

Chapter 4: Mom Guilt

This can be a touchy subject for a lot of moms when it comes to entrepreneurship and growing a business for yourself.

Whether your business is your full-time gig or even a part-time "side hustle," one of the biggest questions I get asked is "How do I do this and not put my kids on the chopping block?"

The "Mom Guilt" we get when we leave our kids or put them in front of the TV while we make our calls, do our meetings, or anything that needs to be done for our business is enough to make any of us want to quit entrepreneurship all together.

Because you've probably been taught there's going to be a short-term imbalance in order to get your business off the ground, you sacrifice some of the most precious moments in your kids' lives for the business and it rips your hearts out piece by piece...

Listen, I totally get it.

My first couple years in entrepreneurship I thought I had to choose between being a successful business woman and being a present mother.

I remember people that were much more successful than me telling me that in order to reach the top I had to make sacrifices.

Which meant missing family activities and not taking family vacations... Putting business first for just a little while... You know, giving up time now to have all the time later.

And that's what I did...

With the end result in mind, I would hop in the car and travel to prospect or do meetings for the business... telling myself it would only be for a few months and then my kids would be put first again.

At the time, we were broke, living in Whit's mom's basement... And sometimes we were traveling 7 or 8 hours one way, which meant sleeping in our car in a Walmart parking lot because we couldn't afford a hotel room... Or finding a place to pitch a tent in the middle of November.

There was no way I was going to do that with my babies... So I thought it was better for them to stay home with Grandma or a babysitter.

The Mom Guilt would eat me alive as I was away from them sometimes for days at a time.

Whoever had them would send me videos and pictures of all the fun they were having at the swimming pool, on 4 wheeler rides, camping, jumping on the tramp and running around playing with cousins, smiling, laughing...

My heart would ache because I wasn't there. I was missing it. They were growing up before my eyes in text messages.

And after 2 years of hustling and grinding this way with very little results or money to show for it...

We were still living in the basement and we were spending WAY MORE money a month than we were making...

I couldn't do it anymore.

I had given up so much time with those boys. Time that I could never get back... All because I was fed some bull shit line that in order to be successful I had to sacrifice time with the 2 things that were everything in my world.

Girl, I'm here to tell you that you CAN have both...

A successful business AND the time and relationships you want with your kids and spouse.

I made the decision in January 2016 that I was done leaving my kids. I was done sacrificing the time and moments I had with them.

I had a heart to heart with Whit and told him we had to figure out a way I could have the best of both worlds... Or I was done.

And if you're a working mama... The pressure is on you even more.

You're at work all day, building someone else's dream, and then you come home hoping to get to work on your dream, only to turn around and see your kids are another foot taller... Another year older...

The baby is crawling and then walking and you start questioning... "Is It Really Worth It?"

Then you feel guilty again, because you know if you don't build it... No one will. And you want that better life for your family.

But it doesn't have to be this way!

Even now that I've found what many would call success and we've created a pretty awesome life for our family... I ask myself, "If I had to do it all over again, would I do it differently?"

The short answer is YES! I would do so many things differently.

Because my first 2 years in this industry were spent making plenty of mistakes and missing out on a TON of moments I'll never get back with my kids... And no amount of money or success can ever replace those moments I missed out on.

So if I was ever given a Delorean and was able to get it up to 88 miles per hour and go back in time I would in a heartbeat...

And then I'd smack myself upside the head and teach myself 2 concepts that are the key to me having both the successful career that I wanted and the deep, strong relationships I now have with my children and spouse... They are:

1. Talking To The Right People
2. Becoming A Master Of Your Calendar

In the next few chapters, we're going to dive deep into these topics... My goal is that you will not only walk away with an understanding of them, but also have a game plan to start putting them into action in your own business.

Because if you choose to commit to mastering them in the next 90 days, you'll look back a year from now and be blown away by the progress you've made in your business, without missing out on time with the people that matter most to you.

Let's get to it.

Chapter 5: Stripping & Meat Smokers

After Whit was laid off from his Dental Tech gig for the first time, he sold cars for about a year at a well known dealership in the next town over...

Because he hated the stigma that came with the title of "Used Car Salesman", he was always transparent and honest with people that came in looking for vehicles.

Choosing to be honest and not lie to people just to get a sale would result in both good and bad months in commissions... Forcing us to live paycheck to paycheck and save any leftover money from good months so we had enough to get through the next bad month.

Over time, he started to grow a small clientele that would refer people to him. He found that those who came in that either knew him, or were sent to him by someone they trusted were much more likely to buy a car than a stranger that wandered in from off the street who was just browsing.

Furthermore, if someone knew him, and had seen an ad for a specific car they knew they wanted before walking into the dealership, they were almost guaranteed to buy it before leaving the dealership.

I've found over these last few years that the following 2 things are key to having people buy from you or join you in any business quickly... Influence and Desire.

A major mistake I see a lot of aspiring entrepreneurs make, that keeps them stuck and frustrated, is assuming everyone wants what they've got.

It's especially common in the network marketing and direct sales space... And even though it's taught by leaders with good intentions, as a hope to get their teams to take action... It can cause a lot of people to break down and quit the industry rather quickly.

You've probably heard it too... The "3-foot rule" as most leaders tend to call it. Everyone that comes within 3 feet of you is a prospect. If they breathe air, they're your perfect prospect.

Everyone that has skin needs your skincare, anyone that eats food needs your health supplement... Everyone needs good credit so they want your financial service... And so on...

While it may be true that your product CAN help anyone with skin or CAN benefit everyone's health... That doesn't mean that everyone WANTS whatever it is you're selling.

And if you've ever tried selling something to someone that doesn't believe they need or want what you've got... you will crash and burn quickly.

It's like trying to sell meat to a vegetarian... Or trying to sell funeral plans to a 20 year old.

It took me too long to figure this out... My first 6 months in business I talked to EVERYONE I knew and everyone that I met about the products I was selling. And even though my products were great and had amazing science behind them that proved they helped people, I didn't have a single customer buy.

I had a lot of friends and talked to a ton of people - hundreds in fact. But because I didn't have any influence over these friends... I got a lot of nos and "let me know how it works out for you."

After burning through my warm market, for the next 18 months, if you breathed air and had a pulse, you could guarantee I was figuring out a way to put my business in front of you, because in my mind everyone wanted to make more money, so they were all my perfect prospects and needed to hear about what I was doing.

In fact, for a short period of time, Whit's and my weekends were spent driving to bigger cities to prospect people at malls, Walmarts, Starbucks, etc... Anywhere with a crowd of people that couldn't run away from us, so we could make small talk and get their information to show them business later.

One time in particular we went south and were prospecting the Las Vegas Strip near the Bellagio Fountains when I met a lady that was local to the area. We'll call her Amy. After getting to know her and learning more about her family, what brought her to Vegas and hearing her mention she was a dancer at one of the clubs near the strip, I knew I needed to prospect her for my business.

She was incredibly outgoing and super friendly... I thought she'd be a perfect fit for my team. So I led with my icebreaker line, "Do you keep your options open when it comes to making money?"

To which Amy replied, "I'm always open to making money." And with that I thought it was a done deal... She was going to eat it up, join my team and we'd fly to the top of the company with the snap of our fingers.

But after about 10 minutes of talking, she interrupted me and asked, "Wait, is this one of those pyramid things? Oh honey, you could make so much more money strippin'."

[Insert Flush Faced Emoji here! haha]

Turns out, when Amy mentioned she was a dancer, she meant *Exotic* Dancer... And she was making about $20K a month with her own stripping gig down the street... And a quick turn of conversation ended with her trying to recruit me into stripping at her club instead of joining me in my network marketing business! LOL

For about a half a second, thinking about the $9 I had in my bank account at the time, I ALMOST thought it might be a good idea to take her up on her offer and make a few bucks so we could afford a hotel room that night! LOL (Totally Kidding...)

But it did cause me to immediately refocus on my original dream of entrepreneurship, the dream that didn't require me to take my clothes off and dance for people I didn't know.

I still talk with Amy every now and again... She's become a good friend... And we joke as she still tries to recruit me into stripping at her club. I laugh, and reply that she can't afford me.

But, this is a good example of prospecting someone that can benefit from what you have to offer... But has no DESIRE to get what you have. Just like Amy had no desire to build a network marketing team, I had no desire to become a stripper... And it didn't matter what either of us said to each other, neither of us were going to join the other.

There are definitely people out there who are actively seeking what you've got though... And it wasn't until I started learning more about marketing and human psychology and behavior that I was introduced to the concept of a Customer Avatar and a Target Market.

The facts are, very few people are actually considered your perfect prospects to begin with... And many of the people that are considered perfect prospects won't be quite ready to buy or join you at this specific moment in time.

And if you don't have any influence to begin with like me, you're going to be going from person to person, spinning your wheels, beating yourself up, wondering what the heck is wrong with you until you either quit or choose to do something different.

Am I right? Or am I right?

The good news is, when you focus on talking to the right people about your business, product or service, they're much more likely to buy... Especially if you can establish trust beforehand... Just like Whit did when selling cars.

And even though the pool of people that want what you have to offer is smaller... there's still thousands if not millions of people that fit the description... You just need to know where to find them and how to attract them.

The point is to focus on talking to the RIGHT people that are looking for what you got... Which means you need to start growing a targeted audience.

If you own a brick and mortar, or rely on the local population around you to buy your products or services, how you grow your audience may vary slightly compared to someone that is international and growing a business online.

Either way, the concept is the same and the smartest thing you can do is start growing the asset of a list... So you have hot prospects to market your goods to every day.

How exactly does this work? Well, Whit has always wanted a good BBQ grill or meat smoker to put on the porch so we could invite family and friends over on holidays for ribs or a good steak on a Sunday afternoon.

A couple years ago when we were still living in our apartment, I started researching smokers and grills by visiting different websites to get an idea of the choices I had that were out there... so that when I was ready to buy, I'd know exactly which one to get him.

I ended up on different lists and started receiving emails from CampChef, Traeger, RecTeq, Etc. Since then, the different competitors have been sending me deals, discounts, and education around why I should buy their type of grill or smoker.

Getting 1 or 2 emails a week, I started leaning more and more toward a Traeger because of the different videos, recipes and other value based content they shared with me. I started to believe that a Traeger was superior to all the other grills that were out there and this past Father's Day, I bought Whit the largest size they had.

Now, I can't say whether or not a Traeger is actually the best meat smoker in the world, but what I can say is they did a dang good job painting a Traeger as the winner... They had honed in on the dreams and desires of a wife that wanted to give her husband the perfect Father's Day gift that he'd been wanting for years.

And when I was ready to buy... It was the easiest decision to buy the Traeger because of all the value they had given me up front over the years... And Whit and I are extremely happy with our purchase every time we have guests over for dinner.

Keeping this in mind, when I first opted into the email list and became a lead for the Traeger company, I wasn't ready to buy yet. The smartest thing they did was capture my info and provide value until the day I was ready to buy... Because at that point, I was the hottest prospect they had.

The same is true with your business. I've learned there's a very big difference between a lead and a hot prospect. A lead is a lead is a lead is a lead...

If you're walking around outside on the street, everyone that you pass can be considered a lead... Because you can have a conversation with them and see if they're interested in what you've got... And then sift and sort them where they go depending on what they're looking for.

Well, it's the same thing online... There are leads everywhere. Your Facebook friends or Instagram followers, people that respond to one of your posts, and even those that request more info from you, aren't yet considered hot prospects...

They're just a lead at that point because they haven't qualified themselves enough to be considered a hot prospect...

A hot prospect is someone that takes action. Someone that goes through a funneling process and identifies themselves as interested in buying your product or service or joining your team right now.

Remember what I said about the ultra successful guarding their time? Well, this also means they're very selective about who they give their time to. And a prospect has to prove that they're higher quality in some way or another in order to get a piece of that time.

When I figured this out... Everything changed in our business... Because I was no longer dealing with tire kickers, dead beats, and time wasters. Instead, I was having higher quality conversations with higher quality people that wanted what I had... And showed that they were ready to buy from me or join me right now.

In case you haven't figured it out by now, people don't like being sold to - especially on social media and in their personal feeds. Because they go to Social Media to be social, they see people hounding them to buy their stuff as an intrusion of their personal space. However, people LOVE to buy when they believe it's their idea...

Think back to Whit selling cars... If someone came into the dealership just browsing and had no idea what they wanted and didn't know when they were going to buy, it was an uphill battle for Whit to sell a car to them...

On the flip side, if someone knew Whit and knew what car they wanted, it was a done deal.

A big problem that I see a lot of aspiring entrepreneurs make is they are always going for the sale. They don't lead with value. Their message is very in your face, salesy, spammy... You know, "buy my product", "join my team" and the problem with constantly sharing content like this is you actually end up repelling a lot of the prospects that you're trying so hard to attract.

So, what can you do to attract those high quality people instead of being the salesy spammy person that's always talking about what they're selling?

The answer might seem vague, but it's actually the first step to building an audience of perfect prospects.

Provide value. That's the answer... Just like Traeger did for me for almost 2 full years before I ended up buying a Traeger. But how do you do that?

Basically, you want to share content that empathizes with your prospects' pain points and desires, making it about them and not about you.

You can do this by teaching, nurturing and inspiring... I like to think of it as edutainment... Educating people while entertaining them with the content you share.

To make it simple, providing value and sharing value based content is what is going to make you attractive to your ideal prospects. It's also going to set you apart from all your competitors that might be selling something similar to you.

So where are these perfect people for you? And how do you attract them?

First, we need to narrow down who your perfect customer or recruit is by identifying what their specific pains/problems and dreams/desires are. And to stick with marketing language, we're going to name and label this person your "Avatar" from here on out.

When thinking about your Avatar, the one that would buy something from you right away without objection... Or join you in your business venture without thinking twice... Ask yourself:

What pains do they have right now and what problems can you help solve?

What dreams and desires do they have that they need your product/service to achieve?

What questions of theirs can you help answer? How do you relate to them?

What is unique about what you have? Why should they give a poop about you and your product/service?

What makes your product/service different from what they've tried in the past?

When I'm sitting down and I'm thinking about my own avatar and what I can share that will attract them to buy a product or service I provide, I'm asking myself what is valuable to that avatar right now? What is going to help them maybe have a better day?

What can I teach them that will have them open their mind to the possibility of something different or maybe joining me or buying a product or service I provide?

Answering these questions and filling in the following chart will help you really get to know your Avatar so you can attract them to you and sell or recruit with ease.

If you're trying to sell skincare products, your Avatar will be different than if you're trying to sell a weight loss product. And if you're trying to recruit someone into your sales team or network marketing team, your Avatar will be different than if you're trying to sell a product.

Pains/Problems	Dreams/Desires	Solution	Language

(You can download a printable copy of this chart at www.yougotthisgirlbook.com/resources.)

I'm going to quickly explain each column of the chart so you get how it works. When working with students, I've found the easiest way for them to get in touch with their Avatar is to think about who they were before they found the product, service or opportunity they're promoting... Because chances are, your perfect prospect is going through the same things you were at that time.

First, the Pains/Problems column will be filled in with the pains, problems and struggles your perfect prospect is going through right now. If you're selling skincare, some of these things could include acne, scars or dark pigmentation, which leaves them feeling embarrassed, caking on makeup to hide their imperfections and spending huge amounts of money trying to find a solution...

The Dreams/Desires column will be filled in with what they want or wish they could have in place of their pains and problems. So thinking about skincare, they might wish they had clear skin so they didn't have to cake on makeup to hide their imperfections everyday... They may have a desire to have dark marks fade or a simple, inexpensive skincare routine that leaves them with glowing skin. They want to look younger, which will leave them feeling more confident in their own skin.

The Solution column will outline how your product, service or opportunity will help bridge that gap between your avatar's Pains/Problems and Dreams/Desires. Keeping with the skincare theme, maybe your product has a patented ingredient that helps fade dark pigmentation quickly... Or maybe the combination of the products you sell can help with fine lines, wrinkles or acne... The idea is to think about how you can educate someone around your solution, so they can see how your product or service is a no-brainer for them to try.

The Language column is there to help you identify the specific language your Avatar uses every day. This way, you can write or say the things that will help your marketing message be really clear and speak directly to the heart of your prospect. So when you write a post, ad, email, or video, you have people responding and reacting because they FEEL your words.

The language our skincare avatar might understand may include Acne, breakouts, wrinkles, dullness, dryness, oily skin, droopy eyelids, Melasma, hyperpigmentation, etc.

To make sure you really understand this, here's an example of another Avatar for a health and wellness weight loss product... Let's say your perfect customer (Avatar) is someone looking to lose weight. Well, the phrase someone looking to lose weight is pretty generic... So let's get more clear on who we're talking to...

A stay at home mom with 3 kids that wants to lose between 25 and 50 pounds of baby weight. Much clearer... And easier to fill out the chart.

The idea is to fill in the chart with every single pain/problem, dream/desire, solution and piece of language you can think of when it comes to your avatar. This way, you can always reference your chart for any marketing project you're about to tackle... keeping your thoughts organized.

Pains/Problems	Dreams/Desires	Solution	Language
-Doesn't fit into jeans -Has a spare tire she can't get rid of -Tired/no energy to keep up with her kids -Hates being intimate with her husband because she's embarrassed of her body -Hitting the gym with little results -Lypo/ mommy makeover isn't possible because of finances	-Fit back into her favorite pair of jeans -Lose the extra flab in her midsection -Run around with her kids at the park -Look good and be confident in her bikini -Have sex with the lights on and not be shy or embarrassed -Feel good about the progress she's made with weight loss	-Gut health supplement that helps stop new fat cells from forming -Clinically proven to shrink your waist -Immediate boost in mood and energy -Whatever else your product is proven to help with and do	-Fat -Tired -Mom Pooch -Overweight -Pounds -Inches -Scale -Gym -Workout -Diet -Exercise -Bikini ready -Slim -Mommy makeover -Hormonal weight gain

An example of how I might use this chart to write a post or do a video promoting something to our weight loss avatar would look like this:

"I gained 38 extra pounds when I was pregnant with my baby boy and it stuck around after he was born. Not only did I NOT feel attractive, but I was so tired from carrying the extra weight I couldn't keep up with my 3 year old.

I tried dieting, hitting the gym and eating healthier, but nothing seemed to be working... I was so frustrated and cried to hubby because I just didn't feel beautiful. I hated being intimate, because I wasn't confident in my own body anymore.

I didn't know that this was a common thing for women dealing with my health condition. It's because of such and such hormones, my body holds onto the weight and won't let go.

I was starting to look into getting a mommy makeover, which was going to cost thousands of dollars, when I ran into my friend Jen at the grocery store last month. Jen looked amazing and told me about a supplement she started taking that was targeting the fat in her body.

I didn't realize I had been missing (ingredient in product) so figured I'd give it a shot. I started taking it a few weeks ago and to my shock I've lost 15 pounds! It's literally melting off me.

This is WITHOUT dieting, hitting the gym harder, or changing anything in my regular routine. I'm so amazed!

If you're struggling to lose those few extra pounds you need to try this stuff... I'm so excited to actually look good in a bikini just in time for summer and I just tried on my favorite skinny jeans I bought before finding out I was pregnant with baby boy and they fit!

This stuff is legit. Shoot me a message and I'll send you the deets."

Now this story isn't my own... It's one I quickly made up... But you can see how I've taken phrases from the columns to craft the message.

By being vulnerable and sharing it in the form of a story, it's like a trojan horse, and you'll hit the heart of your prospect... Which will feed their desire to buy whatever it is you have even more.

Now, take a few minutes and fill in the chart with your own Avatar.

Get as detailed as you can in each column. What are the specific pains, problems and struggles they're going through right now?

What dreams or desires do they have?

How does your product, service or opportunity bridge the gap from their pains/problems to their dreams/desires?

What phrases or keywords would they hear and know exactly what you're talking about?

The more detailed and clear you get around your avatar, the easier it will be to speak to them and have them hanging on your every word.

Chapter 6: The Lifeblood Of Your Business

Now that you've filled out your chart and have a good idea around who your avatar is that you want to attract... The next question we need to answer is where do I find these prospects to attract them?

Growing a targeted audience or "network" and having new eyes on your offers is the lifeblood to any business. Because girl, if I've learned anything these past few years, if you aren't growing, you're going backwards.

Even those people you know with influence that are able to grow big businesses quickly will eventually get to the point where they plateau if they don't have a way to attract new prospects, customers or clients each day.

In fact, I got a Facebook message from an old friend of mine that is a top earner in a well known direct sales company... We'll call her Teri. A few years ago, she had a thriving business with a team of a couple thousand... Business was amazing and it was her and her husband's bread and butter.

When I first started in the network marketing space, I bought several of her products and even took a look at her company to see how she had grown her business so fast...

She had built the entire thing using old school strategies and found a few people that had influence, making it pretty easy for her to fly to the top of her company quickly.

But since I didn't join her team and we both went on building our separate businesses, we had sort of lost touch over the past few years. Come to find out, her business had hit a major roadblock when COVID hit and her check dwindled fast over that year... Dropping from over $20K a month, down to under $10K.

It made sense when I thought about it...When you rely on in person meetings and home parties to grow, social distancing and lockdowns can really throw a wrench into things.

Teri was stressed... As I'm sure you can imagine. She had become accustomed to a certain lifestyle and was going to have to sell her home if something didn't change fast.

She knew that I did a lot with Social Media and wanted to run some ideas by me. After 10 years in this industry she was sick and tired of prospecting her same friends and family to host parties and join her business...

I can't say I blame her. In fact, I came to that conclusion myself in January 2016. After talking with her, I was reminded once again, that most people don't focus on connecting with and growing a targeted audience of people that want what they have to offer.

So their revenue is volatile, constantly fluctuating with no way to continue growing or scaling past where they're at.

Now when it comes to growing a targeted audience, there's more to it than just putting up a website and waiting for the phone to ring off the hook or your inbox to explode with people wanting to work with you... Which is what Teri believed would happen before our conversation. What she failed to see is that without a constant flow of NEW people visiting your website or offers, putting a website together is all for nothing.

Now before I go any further, I want you to know you absolutely CAN get high quality prospects reaching out to you. I have it happen every day via email, private message and phone calls... Big name brands like Walmart, Coca-Cola, and McDonalds all understand this and have people seek out what they have to offer everyday.

But it takes a little bit more than simply telling people what you do or what you've got.

There are actually 2 different ways you can grow an audience and depending on your business model, you have a choice of whether to use both ways or just choose one or the other. They are organic (free) strategies or paid advertising.

Big name brands like the ones I just mentioned, spend hundreds of thousands if not millions of dollars each year advertising what they've got for one purpose... To get more eyes on their offers and keep their brand at the top of the consumer's mind. Because the more you see them, the more likely you are to visit them when you're in need of their products or services instead of their competitors.

Both organic and paid strategies work. No doubt about it. The difference between them is how fast you want your audience to grow. Using paid advertising like social media ads and press releases will cost money up front, so it's important to make sure you aren't spending more than you're making AND it's important to understand the process if you hire it out, so you aren't given a run for your money by someone that isn't getting you the results you should be getting.

But it's also important to keep in mind that there's give and take in everything. Free strategies are not necessarily free. What you don't spend in money you'll make up for in time and effort.

Even if you plan to use free strategies to grow your audience, chances are it's still going to require an investment of time, money, effort and energy at some point to reach the top of your industry.

The best thing I ever did for my business was invest in a mentor to show me how to grow rather than continue trying to figure it out myself. Because had I not hired that mentor, I can guarantee I wouldn't be where I am now. Chances are, I'd still be in my mother in law's basement... Or back to working a 9-5.

A common argument I hear from a lot of people when it comes to spending money on personal growth or spending money to learn something new is "Oh I'll just learn that off free YouTube videos."

Excuse me, what? You really expect to grow a million dollar business without investing a dime?

Girl, I hate to break it to you, but that ain't possible... At Least I've never personally met a millionaire that didn't spend money to make money at some point. I always tell those people to come talk to me in a year, when they're still stuck in the same place they are now, and we'll revisit the conversation! LOL

Even doctors, lawyers and other high paid professionals spend thousands of dollars in schooling to learn their skills... And that's just the beginning. That doesn't include the amount of money they spend to keep their practices open.

Long story short... Success requires investment. Investing in your skill sets, investing in your mindset, investing in inventory or investing in software... Whatever it may be, it usually takes money to make money. And once you can be okay with that, decide what strategy you want to use to connect with new people every day that want what you have.

If you do decide to use organic strategies, understand that it may take longer to reach the top than someone paying for services that get new people in front of them daily.

I'm not saying that paid advertising is better than organic strategies. I actually use BOTH in my own business... Because in order for me to coach entrepreneurs effectively, I have to stay up to date on what's working...

But what I am saying is to find a strategy that works for your industry and your groove and stick to it when you get it working. No matter what strategy you choose, it will probably take some time, testing and tweaking... And there's usually a learning curve anytime you start something new... But that's what evaluation is for. So you can speed up the process to getting the results you want.

And if you do decide to try something new, I recommend finding someone that's using the strategy you want to use right now to grow and have them show you the way.

John C. Maxwell said it best when he said, "A leader is one who knows the way, goes the way, and shows the way." Well, a good mentor does the same. If you do decide to find a mentor, expect it to cost money for them to teach you.

Never expect anything for free. You usually get what you pay for in business and in life. And if you're a network marketer and think your upline will teach you for free, remember... Your upline makes money off of you being successful... So it isn't "free" for them to teach you after all. And that's a GREAT THING.

Because just like you expect to pay a good doctor what his skill sets are worth when you or your child are sick...

Or you expect to pay a good pilot that's about to fly the plane you're boarding through a winter storm...

Paying a good mentor what they're worth to teach you the skill sets they've developed and the knowledge they have around the strategies you want to use is worth every penny.

If you're worried about finding the perfect mentor, ask yourself if the strategies they use are in alignment with how you want to grow your business and live your life. If they are, jump in and commit to the process. Even if it takes you 2 or 3 tries to find the right one, it's still worth it when you do find the right one.

Understanding WHO you want to attract, WHERE to find them and HOW to attract them to you is the lifeblood to your business. I'm so passionate about this, I always spend extra time with my clients & students in this area because it sets the foundation for the rest of your business.

If your business hits a standstill or you're having trouble getting it off the ground, take a look at how many new prospects you're connecting with each day. How many new eyes are on your offers? And more important than that... How many of those new prospects fit the description of your avatar?

Chapter 7: The Master of Your Calendar

So where do you spend your time?

Let me make sure I'm clear when talking to you about this subject...

Time cannot be managed. We all have 24 hours in a day. And unless you actually have the keys to that Delorean we talked about earlier, the same goes for you too.

The difference between people that have figured out how to have the best of both worlds and those whose business is suffering or their relationships are on the rocks as they try to build their dream is how they prioritize their tasks each day...

And where they choose to put their time, effort & energy.

As you start to find success in your business, you'll start to connect and become friends with more and more people that are successful...

Have you ever heard the saying you become like the 5 people you spend the most time with? This is absolutely true! Like attracts like... And successful entrepreneurs tend to gravitate and find other successful entrepreneurs.

One thing I've found after countless conversations on this subject is that the ultra successful are extremely disciplined with their calendar and strictly guard their time.

The majority I've talked to have gotten really good at finding a groove for themselves and their families that allows them to make the space needed to build a big business, as well as set aside the time they want/need to spend with their children and spouse.

Now early in my career, the advice I would have given you on this subject would be to sit your kids in front of the TV all day or hire a babysitter to keep them entertained while you work.

Though this may be advice that can work for short-term sprints, it's definitely not fit for building a long term and sustainable business... Especially one where you don't miss out on your kids' lives in the process.

This is why it's important to schedule time with your kids & spouse FIRST!

I want you to open up your calendar right now so we can create a schedule that works for you... (A printable calendar can be downloaded at www.yougotthisgirlbook.com/resources.)

Let's take a look at the next 7 days.

Everyone has non-negotiables in their calendar that you can't change. Some of these things include sleeping, eating, your full or part time job, etc. Whatever time is leftover after these non-negotiables are scheduled, becomes your working calendar and schedule.

Take a few minutes now, and pencil in the family time that also counts as a non-negotiable for you, that you don't want to miss. This can include ball games and dance recitals... Family camping trip coming up? Schedule it in... Your son's birthday party? Put it in... etc.

What are the family events that, if you miss, might make you resent your business? Or drive a wedge between you and someone you care about?

It's crucial you nail this down... A dear friend of mine and business partner spent the first few years of her entrepreneurial journey putting her business ahead of everything else. We'll call her Sarah. Sarah wholeheartedly believed that the short-term sacrifices she was making would be worth it to have the long-term gain she was working toward.

Her oldest daughter tried out and made the drill team her senior year... During this time Sarah was in build mode for her business, and she wasn't using social media or any online strategies to grow. This meant long road trips out of town to meet with prospects, hours spent on the phone, weekends at company training, etc. To this day, there is a big wedge between Sarah and her daughter because Sarah missed 90% of her daughter's games, recitals and competitions that year.

"You chose your business over me"... Is the phrase Sarah's daughter uses to this day...

Now, Sarah is a damn good mother and she loves each and everyone one of her kids deeply. Shortly after this, she made the decision to never put her business in front of her kids again... And has since become a master of her own calendar.

She thought the sacrifices she made back then would only be "short-term"... She was told they would be "worth it." But now, she'll be the first one to tell you not to miss the recital... That no amount of money you make will be worth missing out on the time you have with your kids when they're young.

So schedule that family time now.

Now I know what you might be thinking... "What about my "Results Driven Tasks? I've always been told to schedule them first in order for my business to grow."

You heard me... Scheduling your Results Driven Tasks ahead of your family is a big No No...

How many times have you sat down to make a call or hop on a training course and your kids are climbing all over you, asking you a million questions, and let's face it... driving you a little crazy at times? LOL

Wouldn't it make sense to take care of your kids first, play with them, eat with them, let them get the wiggles out and THEN work on your business for a focused period of time?

Now don't get me wrong... Those Result Driven Tasks are important...

And your business really WON'T grow if you don't focus and take action on them every day.

Which means there may be little sacrifices when prioritizing, meaning you might not be able to kick your feet up and relax all evening binge watching Netflix... Or you may need to cut play time with your kids down from 2 hours to 1 hour a day when you're in "all out massive action" mode.

But if you do schedule your family first, you'll find the time spent on your business is better focused, because you aren't feeling guilty about not giving your kids time... And it will be more productive because your kids won't feel like they're being pushed to the side.

Believe it or not, kids can be trained... I've found even my daughter who just turned 1 will be happier for a longer period of time when we've spent a few minutes eating, playing and snuggling, before I hop on a meeting or do a video for my business.

If you have little ones at home, I promise if you make time for them first, they will be more patient while you work. It may take a little time to get them trained and for everyone to fall into a groove... But your kids are only little once. It's crucial to take a little time out of your day to be present for them now.

That Disney vacation you want to take is going to be a lot more magical when your kids are little than when they're pre-teens and don't believe in the "magic" anymore. Take the damn vacation.

We don't get this precious time back. The memories you make now are far more important than any amount of money you make in the future.

And take it from me, you'll be much happier down the road, even if it takes a little longer to reach a goal, to still have the precious memories and moments with your children... Don't give up everything for the next 2-5 years and look back and say "I missed it."

Now that I've hammered family time into your brain... Let's talk about Result Driven Tasks... because that's what we need to put on our calendar next.

This may look different depending on your business. If you own a brick and mortar, your tasks may be slightly different than if your business is digital and built online... And many aspiring online entrepreneurs THINK they're spending time doing Result Driven tasks when they aren't. Think of Result Driven Tasks as Money Making Actions...

The point is to schedule in the tasks that directly lead to a sale, or if your business involves growing a team, a new teammate. What are the tasks that directly impact and lead to you making money?

When I work with students and teammates that are short on time, I help them break these tasks up into three, twenty minute time blocks. This is the key to success for the majority of the Mompreneurs I coach.

We call it our 20-20-20.

The first block is spent growing your audience. The 2nd block is spent engaging with that audience to build, know, like & trust. The 3rd block is spent promoting & having enrollment conversations.

We'll dive deeper into these time blocks later... So keep it in the back of your mind. But for now, schedule out the tasks you usually do each day to make money. Sales calls, enrollment Zooms, interviews, Live videos on Social Media, etc.

I personally like to break my calendar down to a Daily Mode of Operation AND a Weekly Mode of Operation. Whether you're growing a business on Social Media or you own a brick and mortar, you'll tend to have different Result Driven Tasks you do each day...

Because of this, not only do I ask "What are the most important things for me to get done today?", but I also ask "What do I need to make sure I get done this week?".

An example is on Monday, Wednesday and Friday of each week I'll do a Live Video on one of my social media pages... Which means Tuesday and Thursday might be spent doing a post or an interview somewhere else... But in the event I'm not able to accomplish my live on Monday, I make sure I have 3 lives done that week... Just on a different day.

A few years ago, I sent Whit to pick up Kaetz from preschool because I was busy on Zoom calls with prospects... The school was only a few blocks away, so it usually took about 20 minutes to pick him up and get home.

Getting done with my calls I realized Whit had been gone over an hour and hadn't come back. I called him to see what was going on and our conversation went something like this:

Me: "Hey, where are you? You've been gone a while."

Whit: "At the hospital."

Me: "Ha Ha very funny. Where are you really?"

Whit: "No seriously, I'm at the hospital. I just cut the tip of my finger off in the damn Navigator door."

(Insert gross pic of severed finger sent to me via text.)

Me: "Are you serious?! What happened?"

Whit: "Kaetz walked out the front door so I hopped out of the car to get him and as I closed the door behind me I pinched the tip of my finger in the door... Out of impulse I pulled my finger out fast. Hence, the ripped finger. Will you please call my appointments I have scheduled for later and move them to Friday?"

No matter how well you plan and schedule there will always be days that get hijacked or blow up in your face. Kids get sick, people break bones, power outages cause you to miss Zoom appointments, etc...

The best way to be proactive and prepare for these types of things before they happen is by scheduling time for it in your calendar. We call this Flex Time.

I like to schedule my flex time on Friday afternoons... I guard this time like a mamma bear guarding her cub. This time is there specifically for things that I wasn't able to get done when they were scheduled during the week. If I end up having a great week where I'm able to get everything done each day, my flex time becomes the beginning of my weekend with my kids.

Owning your calendar and being disciplined enough to hold yourself accountable to it will set you up for success.

I was on a Zoom call with a prospect a few weeks ago and I was sharing my screen while giving her some coaching around enrollment conversations and recruiting business builders into her team. When we were done, I opened my calendar to schedule a follow up Zoom with her and her jaw hit the floor when she saw how organized and full my calendar was.

Out of nowhere she started laughing and said, "I don't think I need another coaching zoom next week. After looking at your calendar, I know what is holding me back from reaching my next goal. I'm way too relaxed with my time and need to be more disciplined in getting my shit done."

Jim Rohn once said "Discipline is the bridge between goals and accomplishments."

I used to think that having a calendar and being disciplined with my time would hold me captive and take away the freedom I was trying to create for myself and my family. This was a limiting belief. The second I started being disciplined with my time and schedule was the second I started growing.

I'm now able to give myself permission and the freedom to live in the present moment and enjoy the rewards of my hard work... Because if you're feeling stressed looking at your calendar, you haven't yet mastered prioritizing your tasks.

You get to choose what your life looks like. Choose to be disciplined and create your own freedom... Because remember, being successful is a choice.

Chapter 8: The Missing Link

After trying to grow a team for 18 months, Whit and I attended one of our company's conventions in November 2015. I entered that event feeling down and frustrated. We'd been working so hard for so long and we didn't have a single team member at the event with us.

Spending more money each month than we were making, with expenses racking up on credit cards faster than I could pay them, I was beginning to think entrepreneurship wasn't for me afterall.

As I sat on a hard metal chair in the audience, I watched as teams around me, with leaders that had started after I did, walked the stage and were recognized for earning incentives and ranking up in their businesses.

Then, when they got to the upper ranks of the company, they recognized a woman that was brand new to the company, that put over $100,000 of volume into her business in 19 days. This launched her business to the top of the company where she was making a 6-figure income.

As they recognized her, I turned to Whit and he looked at me and I asked "What are we doing wrong?"

Here we were busting our butts, leaving our boys and missing out on moments with them with thousands of dollars of debt piling up and the only thing to show for our efforts. I knew there had to be something I was missing and I had a feeling this woman was my answer.

I looked her up on Social Media on the spot and started digging into all she shared and offered to try and figure out her secret to growing so quickly... And what I discovered completely changed the way I built my business from then on.

So why do some people seem to effortlessly find new customers or teammates, while others struggle to recruit a soul? Do they know a secret? Were they born lucky? What hidden quality do they have that helps them find success so easily?

In digging into this woman's social media I found that there IS something that some people have up their sleeves that others don't, which allows them to easily sell products, grow teams and make money quickly.

It's an invisible force that's the missing link to you attracting all the prospects, customers, clients or teammates your heart desires.

This magical force is called INFLUENCE.

Here's the thing... If you aren't able to build a little rapport with your prospects or let them get to know and trust you before you hit them over the head with a sales pitch, they're never gonna buy from you and they're never gonna join you.

So, how do you build influence? And how do you do it quickly so that people aren't taking weeks, months or even years to take action on whatever you want them to do?

Think about the last store you visited where you made a purchase or the last product or service you bought online... Chances are, you bought whatever you did because you knew or liked the style or at least had trust that the person or website you bought from would deliver what was promised. If there was no trust or you didn't like the person you were buying something from, you wouldn't have bought it... Am I right?

When a person, business or brand has built influence, they're able to attract leads, customers and team mates with ease.

The good news is influence CAN be built by anyone... Regardless of previous experience or results.

With my students, clients and teammates, we focus on building influence right out of the gate by building a personal brand that helps build know, like and trust with prospects quickly.

If you're building a brand on social media, keep things super simple in your mind by thinking of your brand as the content you share and the stories you tell on your social media accounts and pages.

This is where you let people get to really know, like and trust you by being your real and authentic self.

If you've followed Whit or I on Social Media for any amount of time, you've seen that we're real, raw and open about what's going on in our lives...

We talk about our faith, what's going on in our personal lives and we build our business with our children around us... Where they regularly make appearances on our live videos, causing chaos and laughter at any given moment.

In fact, a couple of years ago, Whit was doing a live virtual Facebook training for a community of about 100,000 marketers...

I was out of town at the time facilitating a 6-figure workshop, helping entrepreneurs scale their businesses, which meant he was holding down the fort at home alone.

Even with 2 little boys playing in the background, Whit found a groove during the training, pouring his heart into the people there and they were getting a ton of value from what he was sharing.

Then, out of nowhere, our boy Zandrix who was 2 at the time, walked over to him and handed him something. Focused on his computer, Whit wasn't paying attention and took it, opened his hand and looked down to find a nugget of poop sitting in the center of his palm!

Zandrix had pooped and decided to share the news with his dad by reaching into his diaper and pulling out a nice juicy nugget so Whit knew he needed a diaper change... In the middle of training 100,000 people! LOL

This was one of the very few times Whit was at a loss for words. He looked at the turd in his hand, looked up at the screen and announced, "Ladies and gentlemen, my son just put a turd in my hand... Please take a quick 2 minute break while I wash my hands and change his diaper."

Now, some people might hear this story and think, "How unprofessional!" "I can't believe he didn't find a sitter." "I wonder what the owners of the community he was teaching had to say about that." And so on...

But the feedback he got after finishing up was the complete opposite. Moms and Dads from all over the world reached out saying it was one of the funniest, most real moments they'd ever watched and that Whit had over delivered on the value!

People expressed thanks with comments like, "If he can deliver a training with poop in his hands, I can definitely do this."

"I don't have to be perfect and can still provide value to my audience."

"It IS possible to grow my business with my children around me."

By being real and vulnerable, you become relatable to all the people you're trying to attract. And you become known for your authenticity, which is one of the most attractive traits you can have as an entrepreneur.

And as you lead with your authenticity and provide value to your audience, you build influence over time. When thinking about what value you can provide to your audience, ask yourself the following questions:

What inspires you and what do you find valuable from the brands you frequently visit?

What can you share that will let people into your life & bless and help them in theirs?

How does your brand tie into the products/company you're building?

Remember like attracts like. If you find something valuable, chances are your avatar will as well. By leading with your heart and coming from a place of wanting to help people, regardless of income, you become attractive to your followers and they become raving fans.

A side tip to keep in mind... Make sure your brand ties into your product, service or opportunity. If you build a brand around horses, but you sell skincare, it can be really hard to bridge the gap from horse to skincare.

Or if you build a brand around goat yoga but the products you sell are in financial services, there's no simple and clean way to quickly turn a follower into a customer.

Instead, make the transition easy by keeping your brand in the same circle of whatever you're selling.

If you build a brand around staying fit and eating healthy, you can easily sell weight loss supplements to a follower.

If you build a brand around good money sense, you can easily recruit a team member into your financial services team because they prequalified themselves by following you over time.

Now, pick 3 to 5 main areas you want to focus your brand on. These areas could be your faith, family, hobbies you have, things you love and things you love to see in your own newsfeed.

My personal brand is centered around my Faith, Family, Digital Entrepreneurship, Travel and Relationships... With random quotes from Friends, The Office and Disney movies thrown into the mix! Haha

The main thing is to be consistent in providing and sharing value... As well as being unapologetically you.

Chapter 9: It Isn't Always Sunshine & Rainbows

The first couple years Whit and I were married, life was pretty simple.

We made decent money as newlyweds and didn't struggle financially like alot of our friends. He was a Dental Technician by trade... The guy that dentists sent their crowns, bridges and full mouth restorations to and he made your mouth pretty before sending it back to the dentist.

We thought life would be smooth sailing. We bought a new house, a new car, a puppy and thought we had it made... Until after a year of trying to get pregnant, I was diagnosed with PCOS (Polycystic Ovary Syndrome) and we found out it would be a lot harder to start a family than we originally planned. This started the Clomid, blood draws, hormone therapy, and more trips to an infertility specialist than I can count.

Then, in March 2011, the dental lab Whit worked for lost their biggest account with UNLV and because he was making the most and had been there the shortest amount of time, he was laid off without warning.

(Talk about a kick in my already broken ovaries.)

He hustled and found another lab to work for, but soon after he was hired, a machine was invented that made it possible for dentists to make their own crowns in house... Over the next 6 months, Whit lost contract after contract and his check went from several thousand dollars a week... To less than 500.

The process of infertility treatments and the different drugs they had me on, mixed with my husband living away from me, was a very low point in my life. The 2nd lab Whit worked for was almost 2 hours away, which meant he'd commute and spend the week living with a couple of our friends up north... Only to turn around and drive home to spend the weekend with me before leaving again Monday morning.

I lived home alone during the week with no one to keep me company but our Pomeranian Chihuahua named Tank ... My parents lived close and I spent as much time at their house as I could, but went through a lot of my constant hormone changes by myself, because I didn't want to be a burden on anyone else.

On the outside I seemed fine. I put a smile on my face and convinced friends and family life was great, keeping my current emotional state hidden from everyone, including Whit and my parents. Whit would call me several times a day and we'd sit on the phone for hours. His calls always had me laughing and happy, but the second we'd hang up, I'd fall back into an abyss of sadness that seemed to engulf me.

I felt like a failure. As a woman I felt I couldn't do the one thing women are supposed to be able to do, my husband was constantly having to call and lift my spirits, and I was selling everything we owned to try and pay our bills.

At this point in my infertility journey, we had had no success becoming pregnant and it was recommended we do IVF. We didn't have any health insurance at the time and were putting the majority of our infertility debt on credit cards.

But after seeing the price tag of IVF and given our financial situation, we declined to start the process and decided to continue doing what we were doing, praying it would eventually work.

Finally in November 2011, Whit knew his time in the dental industry had come to an end, and he found a job closer to home, which was a huge blessing for me and my mental health. This led to him becoming a Jack of all trades to try and keep some type of income coming in while he figured out what he wanted to do for the rest of his life.

And then in April 2012, after 18 months of doctors visits with no success, I decided to quit the infertility treatments cold turkey. I was DONE with the fluctuating hormones and we decided we'd give my body a break and try again when we were in a better financial state.

Stopping my infertility journey was a relief to me. I wanted a baby more than anything, but the process of being poked and prodded, drugged to play with my fluctuating hormones, getting my hopes up with each pregnancy test, only to see the negative sign pop up month after month was more than I could bear. So Whit and I decided that since we were still young, we'd pay down some debt, save up to travel and revisit having kids in the future.

But God had other plans.

It was a Monday morning in June. I had just been hired as a typesetter for the local newspaper in the next town over and I was hurrying to get ready for work. I was feeling like myself again... It had been over 8 weeks since I had stopped the treatments and life was looking up.

New job... New hairdo... and as I opened my bathroom cabinet to grab my hair straightener I saw my box of pregnancy tests sitting on the top shelf. I grabbed my phone and pulled up my calendar to count weeks. I was 5 days late.

Now, I had only had 1 cycle since quitting my drugs cold turkey... And I had been feeling crampy the past week. So I pulled the final pregnancy test from the box, with no expectations other than taking the last test to get rid of the box.

To this day my specialist doesn't know what caused it... He speculated that my quitting everything cold turkey jump-started an ovary... But as I lay that pregnancy test down on the kitchen counter I watched as that test showed a positive sign for the very first time.

I didn't believe it at first. I sat there dumbfounded... Unsure of what to feel or how to act, and then a nervous excitement coursed through me and I called my doctor to confirm that this was actually real.

I'll never forget Whit's face. I took all the clothes out of his top dresser drawer and replaced them with a few onesies, diapers and wipes, and a sign that said "Make Room Daddy, I'm Moving In."

And a trip to the doctor confirmed I was 5 weeks pregnant and we made plans to tell our parents that weekend.

However, our joy was short-lived.

The following Friday morning, only 5 days after finding out I was pregnant, I felt a gush in my underwear. Rushing to the toilet, I sobbed as the blood pooled below me, and I knew something wasn't right.

Whit left work and rushed to the doctor's office where he met me in the parking lot. I was an emotional wreck as we sat together in the patient room, looking at a mural on the wall and reading a quote from Winnie the Pooh on repeat.

"You are braver than you believe. Stronger than you seem. Smarter than you think."

I read it over and over, trying to forget about the blood pooling between my legs in a pad I had put on earlier.

When my doctor walked in, his face said it all. His eyes were full of sorrow as he confirmed I was losing the pregnancy.

Whit brought me home and for the next week I cried, and then I yelled and then I went numb. I blamed myself even though I was told over and over it wasn't my fault and I knew I couldn't have done anything to cause it... I blamed my body. I questioned God, asking "Why would you do this to me?"

"Why make me go through all the infertility treatments, let me quit, and give me a pregnancy, only to take it away?"

During this time, Whit didn't know how to help me. But I wouldn't have chosen anyone else to go through it with. He held me while I cried, allowed me to yell, and together we held tightly to one another, using sex with each other to cope with our sadness and frustration of losing our baby.

Going through this put a lot of things into perspective for me.

My mom brought 5 healthy kids into this world... But what a lot of people don't know is that she had 6 miscarriages in order to get her 5 kids.

The pain she felt as she lost each one of those babies engulfed her in sadness. She always told us that each baby she lost made her love and appreciate each one of us even more. My mom is resilient and so strong... I was fortunate to have her as I went through this first miscarriage. The love and support she was able to give me having been through it 6 times helped pull me through.

And through all the pain and sadness I felt over those 3 years of trying to conceive, I learned a few things that have come to serve me in my business and in life...

First, you never know what people are going through behind the scenes. On the outside they may seem fine... They may seem like they've got it all figured out... Their life is perfect... But on the inside they could be falling apart.

Treat everyone with kindness. Go out of your way to reach out to those you love... Tell them you love them. It might be the thing that keeps them going another day.

Second, if you're in that downward spiral and you find yourself falling into sadness that you can't get out of, Get Help. I am not a doctor and only speak from my own experience, but if you want to break the cycle, you have to be intentional about CHOOSING to do the things every single day to break free.

Even if I didn't feel like it, daily exercise, sunlight, a healthy diet, and connection with other people were things I focused on everyday to start feeling better. Don't be ashamed of your feelings. Reach out to friends and family. Let them know what you're going through... And seek medical advice quickly if things start becoming more than you can bear.

Third, struggling with infertility and building a business are both an emotional rollercoaster. And just like life, building a business never goes as planned. Just as I thought it would be easy for Whit and I to have kids in the beginning, I thought building my business and growing a team in network marketing would be a piece of cake.

Entrepreneurship is NOT easy. You'll experience the highest of highs when things are working and then flip and experience the lowest of lows as things plateau... Come to a halt... Fall apart... Or you even struggle to get things up and going to begin with.

The best thing you can do as an entrepreneur is learn how to manage your emotions so the lows you experience don't give you an excuse to give up.

In any business, things will happen that will have you questioning if entrepreneurship is really for you. But how you choose to react to those things when they happen will make or break your business.

I've found, the easiest way for me to stay the course and continue to keep going each time I fail is to stay in evaluation, celebrate each win no matter how big or small it may be, and vent and problem solve with Whit and my other business partners whenever it all becomes too much to handle myself.

Having people you can confide in, celebrate wins with, and to keep you accountable is a huge advantage to an entrepreneur. If you haven't found those people, I suggest you do that now. Even if it's just one person that you can voice frustration to without judgment, it will help you keep your sanity when times get tough.

Now, let's fast forward to one month after my miscarriage...

Remember how I mentioned Whit and I turned to sex to help us cope with the loss of our pregnancy? Well that turned out to be a huge blessing for us that showed up in the form of ANOTHER positive pregnancy test.

30 days after taking that first test, I took another, because I was feeling the exact same way I felt with the first pregnancy. I was tired, crampy and again, was late. This time I knew I was pregnant before I even took the test... And when that pink positive sign popped up and confirmed I was given another chance at a baby, I was at peace.

I thanked the Lord for another chance at becoming a mother and decided that I was going to soak up every minute of being pregnant and do my best to stay positive and be the best mom to that little baby growing inside me whether we made it to term or not.

9 months later I delivered a healthy baby boy that completely changed my life forever.

Sometimes when things don't happen for us right away, it's not that they won't ever happen for us at all. There's a lesson we can take from each of our trials and painful moments that we can use to fuel our future experiences for the better.

Whit and I ended up having 2 more miscarriages in between our second boy and baby girl. And even though those miscarriages knocked me to my core, I knew I would make it through it... Because I had made it through it before.

Whatever you may be going through right now or in the future that brings your life to a sudden halt, I promise you CAN make it through it.

No matter how painful it may be, no matter how stripped down you may feel, you can make it through it if you choose to. And when you do, you'll come out a completely different person, that's renewed, wiser and capable of making it through anything.

Chapter 10: That Time My Mom Was Right

I have an irrational fear of alligators.

The first time I flew into Florida for a workshop I looked out the window at all the lakes, rivers and pools and immediately began to hyperventilate. My palms started to sweat, my face went cold and clammy, and my business partner Brandy had to remind me to breathe to keep me from passing out on the plane.

I've had this irrational fear for as long as I can remember... And over the years I've done a little digging on myself to figure out where this fear stems from.

As a little girl, my family would take camping trips down to Moab, Utah, where we'd camp near the Colorado river. The river has swift, deep currents that could easily sweep a young kid off their feet in an instant.

To keep my brother, sisters and I safe, my mom would always hammer the following lesson into our brains to keep us away from the river... "Don't go by the river. There are alligators in there. They can walk along the shore. They'll jump out of the water and grab you. Stay away from the river. You'll get ate by an alligator if you go near it."

Now my mom had really good intentions... She didn't want to turn her back and have any of her children swept down the river and drown... The Alligator thing kept us all safe because it kept us away from the river.

But this wasn't the only place my mom used the Alligator line to keep us safe. My Great Grandma in Murray had a ditch across from her house that was about 2-3 feet deep. When my mom was little, one of the neighborhood toddlers had fallen in the ditch and drowned... So my Grandma and Mom always told us there were alligators in the ditch so we wouldn't go near it and fall in.

Again, I grew up in Sandy, Utah, and used to run near the Jordan river every now and again... Anytime I saw the water, I could hear my mom's voice in the back of my head... "Don't go near the water. There are alligators in there."

As I got older I learned there's no alligators in the ditch, Jordan or Colorado rivers... The water and climate is way too cold. But as a kid, I never went near the river, for fear of being eaten... So I never drowned...

BUT, when I was 13 years old, as I sat one summer morning eating my Lucky Charms cereal at the kitchen counter, my mom had the news on... And there, right before my very own eyes, I watched a breaking news story about a damn alligator being pulled out of the Jordan River!

My heart raced... The anxiety set in as I realized Mom. Was. Right.

There aren't supposed to be alligators in Utah... And the news reporter chalked it up to someone getting the alligator as a pet and once it reached a certain size they couldn't take care of it anymore so they set it free in the river.

But the fear I had of alligators up until that point suddenly became irrational... I still can't watch an Animal Planet alligator/crocodile episode without anxiety shooting through my body.

Now to someone reading this who lives near gators and finds them in their swimming pool every now and again might be laughing at me right now over this irrational fear.

But let's talk a little bit about FEAR in general... Because it is a very real thing and it was put in our very DNA as human beings to keep us safe as we were running from saber tooth tigers and dinosaurs. As a human being, that fear of alligators kept me safe from drowning as a small child.

But, some people spend their entire lives running from fear, allowing it to control them and this is when those irrational fears you have will hold you back.

You'll use your fears as an excuse not to do the things you know would better your life...

And so you stay stuck...

Frustrated and complaining that you aren't moving forward.

For entrepreneurs, some of the fears that hold us back might include public speaking, meeting new people, making phone calls, having sales or enrollment conversations, fear of advancing technology, fear of taking risks, fear of success, fear of failure, etc.

Did you know that you actually have total control and a choice when it comes to the fears you have in your life?

Imagine if I had allowed my irrational fear of alligators to control whether or not I attended that first workshop in Florida... Because that first workshop, which was held in a hotel in Orlando right on a lake full of alligators, set the course for me making my first 6-figures in my business.

Now, I had other fears like you when I first started my business. In my natural state I prefer to keep to myself. I'm not naturally a person that goes out of my way to network and meet new people.

Believe it or not I'm pretty shy... And it used to take all day for me to warm up and build the courage to make the phone calls I needed for my business or to prospect the cashier at Walmart as they were checking out my groceries.

But because I feared being stuck in my in-law's basement forever... And feared my husband would be stuck working 16 hour days at a job he hated... I taught myself to feel the fear and do it anyway.

Over the course of a few months and then a few years, I got really good at meeting new people and having enrollment conversations.

You have the power and ability to choose success for yourself... To feel the fear and do it anyway too. Because unless you're being chased by a lion, falling from a building, or in the middle of an event that could take you or a loved one from this world...

FEAR is all in your mind and fear itself can't hurt you.

At that very first workshop I attended in Florida, that shot my business to 6-figures, I learned to ask myself a question anytime I was feeling fear or worried about something I was about to do.

It stems from the word WORRY... Will The Outcome Really Ruin You?

Anytime I was afraid to make a phone call I'd ask myself this question. Anytime I was about to get up and teach from stage... Anytime I felt that fear and anxiety set in that would usually shut me down and keep me stuck.

So let me ask you... What fear do you have that you're choosing to allow control you? What are you not doing in your business that you know you should be?

Because if you keep running away from your fears... You'll stay stuck. As with anything, growth happens outside your comfort zone. The good news is your comfort zone can be stretched like a muscle if you choose to allow it to. The more you choose to face your fears... To feel the fear and do it anyway, you'll find the easier it becomes to do it.

So get EXCITED about facing your fears...

Because the sooner you choose to move through them, the sooner you'll grow and become that person you were pre-ordained to be.

"You cannot find a happy life. It is not something you can trip and fall into. You have to create it for yourself!"

– Cari Higham

Chapter 11: Pivot!

In early 2019, Whit's dad went in for a routine knee replacement surgery to fix a kneecap that was broken. He had his knees replaced before with no issues so we all expected a routine procedure and recovery.

Little did we know, a staph infection that had lay dormant in his body from his first knee replacement years earlier would rear its ugly head and throw a wrench into his recovery.

To treat the staph infection, they put him on a medication he ended up being allergic to... And this started the downhill spiral to multiple organ failure.

In June 2019, he spent several weeks in the ICU and we watched our grandpa and dad fight for his life... Almost checking out and leaving us multiple times.

Because Whit and I worked from home and had the financial flexibility to help where needed, we traveled the 1.5 hours to Provo several days a week to visit the ICU, did what we could to take care of Whit's mom, and held down the fort at home taking care of their house, yard and animals.

I'm so grateful for prayer, modern medicine and the amazing staff at Utah Valley ICU that were quick on their feet and made every right decision to save my father in law's life. We were told by several doctors that had worked in the ICU for 30+ years that he was the sickest man they had ever treated that made it out of the hospital alive.

We're so lucky and blessed to still have Whit's dad with us...

He's been an influence and cheerleader in Whit's life and my kids adore their Grandpa John. This experience, though it had a happy ending, smacked us upside the head with thoughts of our own mortality, which caused us to start putting things in place to build a bigger legacy for our family.

If there's anything I learned from those long few weeks, it is the importance of having STRENGTH.

Strength in body to overcome any battles that might be thrown at you.

Strength in mind to overcome obstacles your body isn't strong enough to get past by itself.

Strength in numbers, because having people in your circle is one of the most important things you can have in times of crisis.

Strength in spirit to carry you through the bad times... And strength in family, faith and prayer.

You never know how strong you are until being strong is the only choice you have. This experience with Whit's dad was the start of several events that forced Whit and me to build strength in these areas.

In October 2019, I found out I was pregnant with our 3rd child after 2 miscarriages and 3 years of trying. My joy was immediately replaced with extreme morning sickness that had me throwing up almost every hour I was awake.

Then in December our family came down with Swine Flu and that was the sickest I've ever been in my life. To have major morning sickness and catch Swine Flu while trying to take care of 2 young boys that couldn't stop pooping or throwing up for 3 weeks straight about killed me.

Even Whit, who never gets sick, was stuck in bed for 2 weeks. And this was only revving up to what we all had in store in 2020... And what a shit show that was!

I think it's safe to say 2020 was a rough year for a lot of people... All we had to do was turn on social media or the news and see that people's hearts and strength were failing them.

With people dying from COVID, suicide rates off the charts, state and national lockdowns going into effect, I personally watched those around me and people I was connected to break down. In fact, 4 people I know and care about took their own lives that year...

For me, I look at 2020 as a refiner's fire Whit and I were forced to walk through... There were alot of things up in the air inside Whit's and my business from the start of the year.

With social media advertising changes and major events taking place leading to us making big changes to offers, products and companies we were promoting, the stress and anxiety of it all really started to weigh on me.

Considering I was pregnant the first 6 months of 2020, my hormones were everywhere as I was dealing with the rollercoaster of entrepreneurship, trying to homeschool my kids when Utah went into lockdown, all while still keeping our home in order.

But to be completely transparent, our house was a mess, my emotions and hormones were a mess, my kids were a mess trying to understand the crazy changes that COVID brought and all I wanted to do every day was crawl into my bed and not come out.

But instead, Whit and I chose to focus on 3 things that set us up to making 2020 our most profitable year yet up to that point...

And even with 2019 being crazy leading up to a crazy 2020, these 3 things flipped our 2020 around and had us end 2020 at an all time high.

Furthermore, we continue to hammer these 3 things into our students, teammates and clients... Because we've found that when they focus on them, they find success.

They are:

1. Being adaptable
2. Doing your 20-20-20
3. Focusing on gratitude

I was 8 years old before I learned how to ride a bike without training wheels. My parents tried teaching me for years before that, but I always refused to try. Then, when I turned 8, I told my dad to take the training wheels off because I was committed to learning so I could keep up with my friends.

I remember the day he took the training wheels off... I had a baby pink and white bike with purple streamers that came out of the handles. It was a beauty. I mounted the pink seat, my dad grabbed the back of my shirt so I could get my balance and I started pedaling.

After a few trips up and down the street, I started gaining confidence... And slowly my dad started letting go so I was riding it on my own. The pride beating out of my chest when I realized I was doing it... I was actually riding my own bike!

We called my mom out to watch my newly found confidence. Again, I mounted the seat, started pedaling and took off. Just as I started to get comfortable, thinking it was easy sailing, my tire hit a pothole and I lost control of the handlebars... Speeding toward the curb I crashed. I crashed hard.

Just like learning to ride a bike, it's inevitable that things will change in your business. Right when you feel like it's smooth sailing... Like you've got it all figured out... You'll hit a "pothole" and feel like you're crashing and burning.

In times like this, it's crucial you let go of the things you can't control and turn your focus to the things you CAN control.

And that right there is probably the most important trait you can develop as an entrepreneur.

By focusing on what you can control, and asking yourself "What Might I Do?" You'll open the resourceful compartments of your brain and you'll find solutions. One of those things you can control is your 20-20-20.

I mentioned this earlier... But Whit and I teach our students and teammates to build their business in three twenty minute time blocks each day.

Throughout 2019 and 2020, Whit and I put this to the test as we tried to take on and balance all the "things" happening to us during that time. By focusing on just being consistent for 1 hour a day, it kept the momentum building even when the world around us was going to hell in a handbag.

So how exactly do you implement the 20-20-20 into your business?

It's simple... Look at your calendar and identify where you scheduled your Result Driven Tasks from our earlier lesson inside the chapter The Master of Your Calendar. These result driven tasks should take up at least 1 hour a day. The great news is that this hour can be split up into three twenty minute time blocks. It doesn't all have to take place in 1 consecutive hour.

The key is to focus on the most important things for those 20 minutes, so you can make the most of that 20 minutes that day.

Your first 20 minutes are spent doing the tasks that directly result in you growing your targeted audience. Some of these tasks might include connecting with people in groups or forums that fit your avatar characteristics... Shooting live videos that you'll turn into ads that will put you in front of new high quality prospects... Or doing an interview in someone else's audience that will get new eyes on you.

Your second 20 minutes will be spent engaging with your audience to build know, like & trust. Some of these tasks might include doing live videos, commenting and engaging on some of your prospect's social media posts, or writing and posting your own posts to build influence.

And then, the third 20 minute time block is spent promoting your product, service or opportunity. Some of these tasks might include having an enrollment conversation and getting people to buy from you or join you, messaging your hot prospects and moving them into enrollment conversations, or doing a live training that has a call to action for people to buy or join.

20 minutes might not seem like a lot of time... But the compound effect that happens from being consistent will result in progress and momentum in your business... And if you want your business to grow faster, you can always focus on your result driven tasks for 2 or 3 or more hours a day. The point is to find a groove that's consistent and stick to it.

Finally, when life happens and nothing seems to be going right... You're riding on that bicycle and feel like you're continuing to crash... Focus on gratitude.

Whit and I welcomed our gorgeous baby girl Demzli into the world at 3:07 in the morning on June 19, 2020. Up until the point of having her, I hadn't had any sleep in 36 hours...

Because of COVID, the only person that was allowed to be in the room during my delivery was Whit... It broke my heart that my mom wasn't able to be there. She was there with both boys so it was a new experience just having Whit and I.

Demzli's birth was fast... I was only in active labor for a few hours before she was born, but it was also very scary.

We knew the cord was wrapped around her neck because of an earlier ultrasound... So my doctor was monitoring her extra closely.

When she started going into distress toward the end of dilation, I'd listen as her heart rate would drop with each contraction. There were a couple times it dropped down into the high 40s when I was pushing and I could see the concern on everyone's face...

In case you don't know, most baby's heart rates are supposed to stay around and above 100 during labor and delivery... So I was terrified... And found myself in fervent prayer pleading she would get here safely.

I had an amazing nurse that could sense my growing fear. At one point, someone mentioned a c-section, but she and my doctor were confident we could get her here faster and safer using a vacuum if I could just dilate a little more in the next few minutes.

So that nurse took it upon herself to make it happen. She reached her hands up inside me and started manually stretching my cervix out. Even though I was only dilated to a 9, her quick thinking to manually stretch me made the room necessary to deliver Demz.

I had her out less than 5 minutes later... 6 pushes total.

We were amazed as we watched as our doctor unwrapped the cord from our baby's neck not just once, but 3 times, and her tiny little body an additional time.

My baby definitely had someone watching over her and we were so grateful her cord was extra long giving her the ability to come out healthy... Because it very easily could have been different.

At this moment, Whit and I chose to focus on what we were grateful for... Even though the experience wasn't what we had expected or originally planned for.

We were grateful Whit was able to be there and I wasn't alone. I was grateful for a skilled doctor and a caring nurse that went above and beyond to take care of me and our baby girl.

I was grateful Demz had an extra long cord so her oxygen and blood supply never completely cut off.

And I was grateful for an epidural that worked well enough that I was able to manage the pain as that nurse reached her hands in me and manually stretched my cervix...

Even though it did lead to a painful and long healing process.

And we were grateful for a healthy baby girl that we were able to bring home to meet her brothers the next day.

It can be easy to focus on all the things that are going wrong and miss the things you can be grateful for in your business and in your life. There have been times in my entrepreneurial journey I've felt slapped in the face, worn down, exhausted and ready to quit...

But with every crappy situation, there's always been some good to come out of it. Sometimes it's hard to find, but if you are intentional about finding something to be grateful for in every situation you're in, you'll find it.

You just had a business partner stab you in the back? Be grateful it happened now and not later down the road when even more of your time, effort & energy is invested.

Your company shut down? Be grateful you're given the space and opportunity to bloom into something new.

You just lost someone you love dearly? Be grateful for the time you did have with them and the memories you were blessed to make in that time.

Does your business feel out of control? Be grateful for the things you CAN control... And focus on that.

It's inevitable your entrepreneurial journey will be a rollercoaster and there will be more obstacles that come up than you want to have to tackle...

But when it happens, choose to be grateful, look at it as an opportunity to recreate yourself, focus on what you can control...

Be adaptable and as good ol' Ross Ghellar from Friends would say "PIVOT!"

"I believe in breathing life into every single day and escaping to a beach any chance you get."

– Cari Higham

Chapter 12: Can You Really Have It All?

One thing I've learned about myself over the years is that I'm a dang hard worker... AND... I love to be lazy.

That might sound like a contradiction... but let me explain...

I can and will outwork anyone at any time...

But, there's nothing more I'd rather do than curl up with my little family on the couch and watch another episode of The Office or Friends for the 300th time.

Let's be real... Anyone would rather spend their time playing than working.

Being disciplined and working hard isn't something that I LIKE doing... But I love the results that come from it and it's something that I've had to train myself to do over the years.

These 2 traits... Hard Work & Laziness... have played key roles in my success.

I've learned to work my butt off in short focused bursts... so I can, in turn, be lazy.

There's a huge myth out there that keeps so many entrepreneurs stuck. So many moms fall into this trap and they end up miserable asking, "What the heck is wrong with me? Why can't I do this?"

They're told they can "Have It All".

Hold my fork, girl, cuz I'm about to get really real with ya. All the #bossbabes out there are probably gonna come at me hard for this one.

But guess what... You can't have it all. There's no such thing as "work-life-balance." It's a LIE.

In order to grow anything worth having... In order to move forward and progress at all... it's going to be very unbalanced for a period of time... And during that time you're going to be stressed, feel overwhelmed, question yourself on every move you make, second guess your abilities, and want to quit.

It may feel like the world is weighing down on your shoulders... And it very well may be at times.

I had this dream and vision to write this book for you. I kept telling myself "one day" I'll write my book. "One Day" I'll become a published author. "One Day" I'll speak on stages and help entrepreneurs crush it in their businesses... And it was always "One Day."

Then, a month ago, I stopped making excuses for myself. I stopped saying "One Day" and I hired myself a mentor to keep me accountable and I started writing.

As I'm sitting here, almost done pouring my heart into these pages, I look back at the last 30 days, because that's how long it's taken for me to get this all out on paper for you... And my life was an utter shit show at times! LOL

In fact, right now, Demz is sitting at my feet eating puffs off the ground... Frozen 2 is blaring in the background... The house looks like a butthole with dishes piling up unwashed in the sink for the last 3 days... Laundry hasn't been done in 2 weeks forcing me to go commando today... I don't remember the last time I washed my hair so I'm rockin' a grease filled messy bun... And I'm on my 3rd cup of caffeine and it's only 3pm.

There has been no such thing as "balance" the last 30 days.

But, as I take a look around and start feeling overwhelmed, I take a deep breath and whisper to myself... "You Got This Girl."

This short-term burst of imbalance is temporary... And the craziness that's taken place over the last 30 days, so I can accomplish this dream of becoming a published author, ain't nothin' compared to what I've gone through to get here.

So no... you can't have it all, because you're human and can't possibly BE it all every second of every day.

You can't be the perfect entrepreneur AND be the perfect mom AND be the perfect wife AND be the perfect cook AND be the perfect housekeeper AND have the perfect toned and sculpted body AND be the chauffeur AND be the butler AND be the next iron chef... And so on and so on.

What you CAN do however, is choose 2-3 things that you're going to be a master in at any given time... And be ok with being mediocre with the rest of it. Because if you only have 2-3 things to focus on, it's much more simple and less overwhelming than trying to be the master of everything.

These people you see that paint the perfect life with the perfect children that always cook the perfect dinners and gleam perfection on social media are only showing you their highlight reel.

I'm reminded of the time Whit and I taught some of our best business building strategies from stage at a social media event in Vegas in 2019. While there we shared the stage with several mentors and influencers we'd been following for years on Social Media.

We were doing pretty well in our business at the time, bringing home multiple 6-figures. But as I networked with these 7 & 8-figure earners I started to feel really intimidated. To be transparent, I thought these people had the perfect life and I began to question what I could possibly have to offer compared to them.

The final day of the event as I sat in the audience learning from the last few speakers, Mike Dillard, a well-known online marketer and entrepreneur was taking questions from people in the audience. A gal that was just getting started in her business asked, "I've heard you become the 5 people you hang around most. How do I get to know and become friends with some of these people that are doing really well that I have on a pedestal?"

To which he replied, "Take them off the pedestal."

This advice struck me deep to my core... Because without realizing it, I had put Mike and several other influencers at that event on a pedestal and it was keeping me back from growth.

So who do you need to take off a pedestal? These people that you idolize and think have the perfect life are human just like you. And whether they show it or not, they struggle and have flaws just like you and me.

SO no... I don't believe in "work-life-balance."

I also don't believe you have to give up the things that matter most to you in order to achieve success.

What I do believe in, is setting boundaries for yourself...

Deciding on a goal and hustling to reach it... but not at the expense of your children, your spouse, or the relationships that matter most to you.

I believe in breathing life into every single day... And escaping to a beach any chance you get.

Or even sitting in the driveway in silence for just a few more minutes before heading into the house to unpack the groceries in your trunk. (If you know, you know. That extra minute or 2 can give you exactly what you need to get through the rest of your day.)

I believe in taking care of yourself... Because I know far too well how much everyone else can suffer if you yourself are broken.

I believe in showing your children they can do & be anything they decide they want to be. I personally want to be the mom that leads by example. That didn't just tell my kids they can do it... But actually show them and live it.

Does that mean I don't lose my shit every now and again? Definitely not. I'm human... I'm building my empire while trying to not just keep my kids alive... But have them grow up to be respectful, honest and hard working people that give back to the world.

And a few more things to get off my chest...

If there is ever a doubt...

Take the trip...

Eat the cake...

Buy the boots...

Be vulnerable and wear your heart on your sleeve...

Rock that baby a little bit longer...

And girl, watch that damn kids YouTube video that junior keeps trying to show you for the 362nd time...

Because they're only young once and the last thing you want to do is look back 50 years from now and say "I'm successful. I have money... But I missed it."

And when life starts to come down hard on you... When you're giving it your all to hit that next goal or create the lifestyle you crave...

When kids are fighting and you're looking around at the messy house, piles of laundry and dishes... When you haven't showered in days and you're resorting to putting puffs on the floor to keep your baby happy for just 5 more minutes so you can finish your work...

Close your eyes... Take a deep breath... And whisper, "You Got This Girl."

Because you do.

About The Author

Cari Higham is a sought-after Speaker, Trainer, and Influence Marketing Strategist that calls Utah home with her husband, Whit, and their three children.

Jumping into network marketing in 2013, she quickly learned that there's a lot more to entrepreneurship than just talking to your friends and family and hoping your business will grow.

Relying on traditional business-building strategies to connect with new people, she struggled for over 2 years to grow her team, driving all over the western half of the United States, prospecting people to join her and buy her products.

Living in her mother-in-law's basement because she and Whit couldn't afford rent while trying to grow their team, she almost quit entrepreneurship all together multiple times. Frustrated by her failing business that was producing less than $100 a month, she put her family further and further into debt as she put all her expenses on credit cards.

It wasn't until she discovered an influence marketing strategy that allowed her to grow a targeted audience through social media and enroll people by the masses, that she started finding success in early 2016.

This strategy shot her income to multiple 6-figures less than 11 months later, which gave her the freedom to move out of the basement, get out of debt and retire Whit from his corporate job.

Since then, she's grown a passion for digital entrepreneurship and helping both aspiring and veteran entrepreneurs alike crush their business goals by implementing simple and effective online strategies to grow their audience, earn more while working less, overcome obstacles, and grow their business using her "1 Hour Per Day" system.

Cari and Whit had the fastest growing team in 2 separate companies, were top earners and affiliates for over 3 years and have built several 6 and 7-figure online businesses, allowing them the time and financial freedom to give back and create a life full of abundance and choice.

In 2021, Cari retired from the network marketing industry to give her the time, space and ability to give back to entrepreneurs all over the world on a bigger scale through public speaking, mentoring and training.

She's a Co-Founder of Beach Boss Influencers, a private coaching community for network marketers, centered in Influence Marketing and Digital Duplication strategies.

She's also helped mold and shape entrepreneurs across the world as a facilitator for 6-figure online marketing workshops over the past 3 years.

There's nothing that brings her more joy than helping entrepreneurs overcome obstacles, smash their goals and create lives of freedom, abundance, and choice.

For public or private speaking events and training opportunity inquiries, please email whitney@whitandcarihigham.com.

Praise

I'm so excited you are getting a chance to read this book. It's been so much fun working with Cari to make her bucket list dream come to reality. When the 'Cari Higham's' of the world come into your life, you might not even realize how blessed you are. I met Cari on a typical Zoom call; lots of faces in the windows and not sure if you'll ever see her again.

Cari knew she had a book inside of her to share with the world and reached out to me for help. Cari is the ideal client you always dream of. She has a passion and a fire that lights up every room she enters and a work ethic of doing what she says she'll do.

When Cari chose her book title, "You Got This, Girl", we knew we had something special to run with. This title isn't just for her book, it represents her mantra for life. Throughout her journey, you can just picture her giving herself a pep talk, "you got this, girl." How often do we mutter under our breath saying the same thing to ourselves? You're going to fall in love with her stories and her passion. You're going to feel like you've got a girlfriend cheering you on, encouraging you to conquer that next hurdle.

Cari pours so much love and passion into others as much as she pours into herself and I'm going to miss our weekly visits. I'll have her book to remind me of this great journey together.

Cheers!

- **Angel Tuccy**, Media Specialist & Best Selling Author

Cari Higham is one of the most gifted teachers and coaches I have ever met. She passionately leads from the heart with joy and humor that's contagious. She has a unique combination of tenacity, grit and elegance that makes her seem almost superhuman. Having worked beside her for many years, it has been an honor and privilege to see her blossom into the influential leader she is today.

- **Tim Erway**, Co-Founder of
AttractionMarketing.com

As a busy entrepreneur and somebody who struggled with time management and living a balanced lifestyle, Caris' methods of building a business in one hour a day has helped me tremendously. I have been able to balance my life out while building my empire without taking away from anything else! Listening to her speak and train completely shifted and transformed the way I do business. I highly recommend any entrepreneur, stay at home mom, or network marketer buy this book as it will completely transform the way you do business!

- **Tina Torres**, The Gratitude Specialist

When I first started working with Cari, she was living in a basement with her husband & 2 kids struggling to buy enough food for her family. Five years later, she and her husband have built a 7-figure business and are living their dreams. This was no accident and I know, because I had a front row seat to their journey and how she did it. My recommendation is you gobble up every word of this book so it can nourish your spirit and income.

- **Ferny Ceballos**, Co-Founder of
AttractionMarketing.com

As a newbie entrepreneur I had the pleasure of attending a workshop that Cari was Facilitating. I was blown away at the way Cari was able to break down complex ideas and processes into bite sized chunks that I was then able to immediately use inside my business. Over the last few years the mentorship and guidance from Cari has been a key component of my growth and transformation as I continue to move forward in my quest to make an impact in the lives of others.

- **Becky Graff**, Coach, Speaker, Author | Co-Founder of TimandBeckyGraff.com

Cari Higham is a powerhouse business woman and heart-centered leader who inspires, educates, elevates and empowers people to be their best. I've had the privilege to see first-hand how she has grown from a hungry student of business and life into a go-to, impactful entrepreneur, trainer, and mentor. She has helped me raise my game and she will do the same for you. Listen and learn from Cari and create the business and life of your dreams!

- **JT DeBolt**, Leadership & High-Performance Strategist

Cari was instrumental in helping me become the leader I am today. From the first moment I met her, Cari made me feel important and that I was her equal, even when she was in a higher position or had more experience. Her focus is always on the success of those she is mentoring and helping. You never feel that she is above you, but rather that she believes in you, and wants to help you become all that you can be. I have relied on her guidance and expertise as I and my husband have forged our own path to achieve our own dreams.

- **Debbie Dunford**, Creator of Expert Online Prospect Attractor Coaching Program | Co-Owner of David & Debbie Dunford

Cari's straightforward, helpful and nurturing style creates the perfect formula for anyone to not just understand her teachings, but to instantly implement them into their own business. Simply put, if you're an entrepreneur looking for a breakthrough survival guide that helps navigate the pitfalls of entrepreneurship and starting a new business... Then 'You Got This Girl' is written specifically for you!

- **Bill Pescosolido**, International Trainer & Speaker | CEO and Co-Founder of The Lido Agency

From the moment I met Cari I could tell how thoughtful and authentic she was. She is down to earth and really understands the ups and downs of entrepreneurship. Because of her empathy, she strives to help people in any way she can to find success. Cari has a servant heart and is always willing to share the knowledge she has gained. Her teaching methods are simple and easy to follow, creating amazing results for those she teaches. Cari knows her stuff and is always willing to share to lift others.

- **Brooke Elder**, Founder of Social Tenacity

You'll be hard pressed to find anyone else who has as much determination, passion and heart that Cari has for impacting others. It's been such a pleasure watching her develop into the Entrepreneur that she is today. If you're looking to kick whatever you're trying to accomplish into high gear... Stop reading this and start digging into Cari's book now!

- **Kate McShea**, Partner of McShea Media | VP of Marketing at AttractionMarketing.com

Cari leads thousands with heart, hard work, integrity, character and more importantly, models a commitment to find balance as a hard working leader, a mom and a wife. Cari brings a wealth of experience and has invested extensively in growing her skills, teaching and training others. She is committed to helping all those she meets.

- **Laurie Proskin**, 7-Figure Network Marketer & Wealth Coach

Cari walks the walk and talks the talk, and has enough real life experience as a mom, wife, and entrepreneur to share meaningful insights on the ins and outs of how to navigate life. She's seen the lowest of lows and climbed her way to an admirable amount of success through grit, perseverance, and a quest for personal development that is 100% genuine. I've known her for over 5 years now, both as a fan follower and later as a friend and colleague, and I've always been inspired and encouraged by both her willingness to be vulnerable and her bravery and kindness as a leader. She is one to follow!

- **Adrienne Hill**, Social Media Business Strategist | Creator of 6-Figure Social Media Sales Machine

Acknowledgments

So many people have been instrumental in my journey and I fear leaving someone out. I'm going to do my best, but if I unintentionally skip over you, please forgive me and know I love and appreciate you more than you can imagine.

First, Whitney, my husband, business partner and best friend. I don't know where I'd be if I didn't have you by my side. You've been a driving force behind my success from the start. Every time I'm frustrated, ready to call it quits and give up on my dreams, you're there to talk me off the ledge, breathe life back into me, and give me the push I need to keep going. To know you is to love you. I've never met anyone more giving of their time and talents and you always know just what to say to keep people laughing. If there's any doubt about the type of person you are, your hashtag given by your students, clients and team mates suits you... #everybodyneedsawhit.

My mom, Christi. Growing up we butted heads a lot. I was stubborn, headstrong and I gave you a run for your money. But, as I've gotten older and experienced more in life, I've learned that you know a lot more than I ever gave you credit for! LOL God knew I needed a strict, but loving mother to keep me on the straight and narrow so I could become the person I am today. I'm grateful for the friendship we now have. You're the first person I call whenever I need help and you're immediately there to love and support me. A prime example was being my proofreader and combing through this book at the last minute. Thank you for everything!

My dad, Keith. Dad, I was blessed to watch an entrepreneur in action my entire life. You were the example I needed to watch and from you I've learned what a work ethic is, how to be tenacious and resilient, and how to set a goal and stick to it. Plus, all those runs we took growing up and the conversations we've had helped mold and shape my mind to think differently than most people. I'll always cherish those moments. There's no doubt, I got my entrepreneurial spirit from you.

Brandy Shaver... Lady, you introduced me to this world. You saw something in me when I didn't see anything in myself. You've been one of my biggest cheerleaders, supporters and accountability partners since day 1. From teaching me how to prospect back in 2013, to partnering up and growing a multiple 7-figure coaching practice in less than 18 months with the Beaches, you've been a rock in my life. I'm grateful for our friendship and that we get to do this together.

My Beaches! Fran, Adrian, Kat, Chris, Ben and Brandy, my business besties... I love you all dearly. The fact I get to work with people that I love while shaping and transforming lives every day is something I always dreamed of creating. The leverage we have by working together makes my spirit soar and I'm excited about what the future has in store for Beach Boss Influencers as we continue serving the network marketing industry and our incredible students.

My siblings, Christin, Halie, Tayler and Austin... I was blessed with the best. The fact I can call any of you at any time and be welcomed with a happy hello is a blessing. My kids have the best Aunts and Uncles a girl could ask for.

Whit's family, especially John & Julie. When life was tough and we needed a place to stay, you welcomed us into your home and allowed us to stay for 2 years... All while we tried to figure this rollercoaster of entrepreneurship out. Thank you for your love and for all the support you gave when we needed it most. Jerold & Wendy, for always being there for us when we need you. My kids are blessed with the best Grandparents and for that I'm so grateful!

Angel Tuccy, this book was only a dream until I met you. As I said on that first call, I don't believe in coincidences! Meeting you when I did was divine intervention and couldn't have happened at a more perfect time. Your mentorship through this process has been priceless as well as your PR services. So grateful our paths have crossed and I've had you to lean on!

Tina Torres, for your expertise in getting new eyes on me, I'm forever grateful. My book will only bless as many people as I can get it in front of. I'm looking forward to continued partnership and growth as we make You Got This Girl a best seller and survival guide entrepreneurs worldwide will reference to grow and scale their businesses.

To my mentors that helped me find freedom...

Tim "TJ" Erway, for seeing something in me and taking a chance on a girl that felt she had so much to give, if given the chance. For seeing my thirst for success and giving me a platform to grow. For welcoming me into your business family circle and allowing me to blossom.

Ferny Ceballos, you knew me when I was at my lowest of lows. Even though I was as broke as broke could get, you gave me the guidance I needed to make the decision of higher level mentorship. That decision changed our lives forever.

Matt Crystal, the care and concern you've brought to my life has touched and changed me. Being able to have conversations without fear of judgment is a breath of fresh air. Thank you for making me feel important and being there in my corner.

Kate McShea, my bestie for the restie! Your belief in me and invaluable insight as I have grown my business has been transformational. Helping me avoid the mistakes you've made while allowing me to pick your brain and bounce ideas off you has helped fast track my success. I love you lady!

JT DeBolt, my brother from another mother... We went through the ringer together to become certified facilitators. Having you as my wingman (and vice versa) as we shifted and transformed lives during workshops for 2 years is something I will cherish forever. Your feedback, energy and commitment to make our workshops worldclass played a huge role in my acceleration of skill sets. I hope we get the opportunity to do it again one day. Come what may, I got your back.

Blair & Melissa Dunkley, the skill sets I developed as a facilitator transformed my life. The processes you taught through mind models have not only made me more effective in public speaking and training, but I now use the same skills everyday with students, team mates, clients and my children. Thank you for working with me and investing in me.

To you, my student and reader. I'm grateful for YOU. Not just for picking up this book, but for having the courage to grow a business and build something for yourself. Entrepreneurs are what keep the world turning. We create the jobs that others fill. Regardless of where you're currently at in your journey, I have no doubt you're going to crush your goals and create the business and life you dream about. I'm confident in this because you're here, reading these words. I hope you've already read the book and you're fired up, taking action inside of your business... If you haven't, now is the time to do so.

And finally, my Lord and Savior, Jesus Christ. My faith has been tested many times over the last few years. But one thing I know for sure... My Heavenly Father loves me, he's heard my prayers and he loves to bless his children. Anytime I've had to make a pivot in my own journey, I've seen the Lord's hand in it. Even when I feel I'm being tested or it feels like things are falling apart, I've seen first hand that they were actually falling into place. Whether you believe in God or not is your own journey. I'm far from perfect, but I've learned the more I lean in and trust him, he's led me to better and brighter things. He never takes something away without blessing me with something better. He loves you... He hears you... He wants to bless you.

Resources

To access all the FREE printable downloads from the book and to get your hands on the additional resources Cari's made available to you as mentioned inside You Got This Girl, go to **www.YouGotThisGirlBook.com/Resources**.

For speaking and training inquiries, permission requests, coaching questions and bulk order purchase options, email whitney@whitandcarihigham.com.